Thomas Holcomb and the Advent of the Marine Corps Defense Battalion, 1936-1941

by
David J. Ulbrich

Occasional Paper

HISTORY AND MUSEUMS DIVISION
MARINE CORPS UNIVERSITY
QUANTICO, VIRGINIA

2004

Other Publications in the Occasional Papers Series

Vietnam Histories Workshop: Plenary Session. Jack Shulimson, editor. 9 May1983. 31 pp.

Vietnam Revisited; Conversation with William D. Broyles, Jr. Colonel John G. Miller, USMC, editor. 11 December 1984. 48 pp.

Bibliography on Khe Sanh USMC Participation. Commander Ray W. Strubbe, CHC, USNR (Ret), compiler. April 1985. 54 pp.

Alligators, Buffaloes, and Bushmasters: The History of the Development of the LVT Through World War II. Major Alfred Dunlop Bailey, USMC (Ret). 1986. 272 pp.

Leadership Lessons and Remembrances from Vietnam. Lieutenant General Herman Nickerson, Jr., USMC (Ret). 1988. 93 pp.

The Problems of U.S. Marine Corps Prisoners of War in Korea. James Angus MacDonald, Jr. 1988. 295 pp.

John Archer Lejeune, 1869-1942, Register of His Personal Papers. Lieutenant Colonel Merrill L. Bartlett, USMC (Ret). 1988. 123 pp.

To Wake Island and Beyond: Reminiscences. Brigadier General Woodrow M. Kessler, USMC (Ret). 1988. 145 pp.

Thomas Holcomb, 1879-1965, Register of His Personal Papers. Gibson B. Smith. 1988. 229 pp.

Curriculum Evolution, Marine Corps Command and Staff College, 1920-1988. Lieutenant Colonel Donald F. Bittner, USMCR. 1988. 112 pp.

Herringbone Cloak-GI Dagger, Marines of the OSS. Major Robert E. Mattingly, USMC. 1989. 315 pp.

The Journals of Marine Second Lieutenant Henry Bulls Watson, 1845-1848. Charles R. Smith, editor. 1990. 420 pp.

When the Russians Blinked: The U.S. Maritime Response to the Cuban Missile Crisis. Major John M. Young, USMCR. 1990. 246 pp.

Marines in the Mexican War. Gabrielle M. Neufeld Santelli. Edited by Charles R. Smith. 1991. 63 pp.

The Development of Amphibious Tactics in the U.S. Navy. General Holland M. Smith, USMC (Ret). 1992. 89 pp.

James Guthrie Harbord, 1866-1947, Register of His Personal Papers. Lieutenant Colonel Merrill L. Bartlett, USMCR. 1995. 47 pp.

The Impact of Project 100,000 on the Marine Corps. Captain David A. Dawson, USMC. 1995. 247 pp.

Marine Corps Aircraft: 1913-2000. Major John M. Elliot, USMC (Ret). 2002. 126 pp.

Occasional Papers

The History and Museums Division has undertaken the publication for limited distribution of various studies, theses, compilations, bibliographies, monographs, and memoirs, as well as proceedings at selected workshops, seminars, symposia, and similar colloquia, which it considers to be of significant value for audiences interested in Marine Corps history. These "Occasional Papers," which are chosen for their intrinsic worth, must reflect structured research, present a contribution to historical knowledge not readily available in published sources, and reflect original content on the part of the author, compiler, or editor. It is the intent of the division that these occasional papers be distributed to selected institutions, such as service schools, official Department of Defense historical agencies, and directly concerned Marine Corps organizations, so the information contained therein will be available for study and exploitation.

FOREWORD

Often historical events are recorded with the benefit of perfect hindsight. That is, the way events end are often considered to have been the way they begun. David J. Ulbrich examined a portion of the Commandancy of Lieutenant General Thomas Holcomb from 1936 to 1943 to illustrate this. When Holcomb took over the Marine Corps it numbered 17,239 officers and men. The Fleet Marine Force consisted of two brigades of 1, 500 men, with no heavy artillery or armor, and about nine squadrons of aircraft. When Holcomb left, the Corps had expanded to 309,559 men and women, with four amphibious divisions, 15 independent battalions, and four aircraft wings. When the war ended in 1945, 485,053 Marines staffed six divisions and five aircraft wings. This exceeded the vision and planning that started the conflict and provided the foundation for today's Marine Corps and its place in the defense establishment.

Thomas Holcomb and the Advent of the Marine Corps Defense Battalions, 1936-1941 examines what General Holcomb had to begin with in this expansion and how he administered and managed the largest Marine Corps increase. Defense Battalions serve as the case study for this examination as they occupied a significant place in the strategic priorities of Holcomb and the Marine Corps during the pre-war era. It is Mr. Ulbrich's contention that Holcomb, more than any other Marine, guided the Corps' World War II mobilization and then directed its participation during that conflict. He functioned as a leader, manager, publicist, and strategist. Holcomb, Ulbrich notes, deserves much credit for forging the modern seaborne service that helped defeat Japan in the Pacific and later distinguished itself during the Cold War.

Mr. Ulbrich is a doctoral candidate at Temple University under Dr. Gregory J. W. Urwin. The work reprinted here was Mr. Ulbrich's Master of Arts thesis at Ball State University. He completed this work in 1996 with Dr. Phyllis A. Zimmerman. Mr. Ulbrich received his bachelor degree at the University of Dayton. He is the author of numerous articles and reviews including "Clarifying the Origins and Strategic Mission of the U.S. Marine Corps Defense Battalion, 1898-1941," which appeared in the October 1999 issue of *War and Society*. Mr. Ulbrich is the 2003 Marine Corps Heritage Foundation General Lemuel C. Shepherd, Jr., Memorial Dissertation Fellow and has received numerous other honors and awards in the course of his work. The Shepherd Fellowship supports research for his dissertation, "Managing Marine Mobilization: Thomas Holcomb and the U.S. Marine Corps, 1936-1943," at Temple University.

J. W. Ripley
Colonel, U.S. Marine Corps (Retired)
Director of Marine Corps History and Museums

PREFACE

First, I would like to thank Professor Phyllis A. Zimmerman of Ball State University's History Department. Her supervision has been truly instrumental in my historical and professional development. From the moment I visited Ball State as a prospective graduate student to the completion of my thesis, Professor Zimmerman has been thoughtful and patient despite my meandering progress and my bad habit of spelling "defence" like the British.

Next, I would like to thank Professors Kevin Smith and E. Bruce Geelhoed, my readers. Their knowledgeable and stimulating comments helped transform my thesis from awkward musings to a more cohesive piece of scholarship.

Next, I would like to thank Lt. Col. E. Lesley Medford, USMC (Ret.), of the 7th Marine Defense Battalion. His contact enabled me to conduct a survey of Marine veterans from the 7th Defense/Anti-Aircraft Battalion. The responses have added color to my thesis.

Next, I would like to thank the Marine Corps Historical Foundation for awarding me the 1994-1995 Marine Corps Thesis Fellowship. This grant allowed me to spend four weeks conducting research in Washington, D.C. Benis M. Frank, Fred Graboske, Evelyn A. Englander, Richard A. Long, Amy J. Cantin, and Charles Melson ably assisted me in my research at the Marine Corps Historical Center. Barry Zerby of the National Archives pointed me toward many classified documents.

Next, I would like to thank several people who provided indispensable support: Glenda Riley, Abel A. Alves, Lawrence Birken, Loren Gannon, Linda Jones Hall, Cynthia K. Thomas, and Cynthia Webb. These people gave me a sympathetic ear, a critical reading, or candid advice as needed.

Next, I would like to thank Professors Raymond White and John Heitmann, former history department chairs of Ball State University and University of Dayton respectively. Both gave me much-needed financial and logistical support during this project.

Next, I would like to thank my father, Col. Richard W. Ulbrich, USAF (Ret.), for many interesting and inspiring conversations about military history.

Finally, this thesis is dedicated to my late mother, Jill G. Ulbrich (1936-1996), who was deeply loved and is sorely missed.

David J. Ulbrich

TABLE OF CONTENTS

INTRODUCTION

PROLOGUE: WHAT IS MILITARY HISTORY?

Throughout history, war has been an integral part of the human condition. Despite apparent advances in civilization, wars still occurred and have merely become more sophisticated with the passing years. Military history is the study of this "organized societal violence." Traditional, "old" military historians wrote about great commanders and grand campaigns in sweeping pen-strokes. They traced the movements of brigades, surveyed the roughness of terrain, and evaluated the leadership styles of generals.[1]

The "new" military history offers a richer, more comprehensive study of war. Broader social aspects of the soldier receive much-needed consideration.[2] Psychological, organizational, and logistical issues also get factored into the military equation. For example, the so-called "grunt" in the trenches receives greater attention. His psyche, morale, and masculinity become fair game for exploration.[3] Interservice and civil-military relations gain clarification through institutional studies.[4] Logistics receives magnified consideration. The military adage "the army travels on its stomach" rings more true than ever.[5] Military history is not limited to the conflicts themselves. The often-tenuous peace between wars must also be investigated.[6] In sum, the "new" military history explores the strategic, tactical, economic, political, social, diplomatic, industrial, and technological effects on wars.

HISTORIOGRAPHICAL VOID

Historians of the Marine Corps have conducted significant research on the development of the Fleet Marine Force's amphibious assault mission. However, little has been written about the evolution of the defense battalion. From 1900 until 1940, advanced base defense's significance in Naval strategy surpassed or equaled amphibious assault. During 1940 and 1941, establishing defense battalions fell to the Corps' second priority.[7] Likewise, few studies have examined Thomas Holcomb. As Commandant from 1936 through 1943, he installed the Corps as the premier seaborne support force and supervised its massive expansion.[8] My study will blend military history with biographical, institutional, business, and political history.

Most histories of the Corps seem to have been written by Marines, about Marines, and perhaps even for Marines. Historians affiliated with the military dominate the secondary scholarship on the Marine Corps. Whereas their association certainly carry definite advantages, these authors also retain biases, prejudices, and sympathies which color their interpretations while not necessarily weakening their studies.[9]

The seminal work on the Marine Corps history is Allan R. Millett's *Semper Fidelis: The History of the United States Marine Corps* published in 1980 and expanded in 1991.[10] While displaying meticulous research and groundbreaking analysis, Millett largely relegates base defense to secondary status in favor of amphibious assault. His book's tenth chapter, titled "The Creation of the Advanced Base Force, 1900-1916," describes advanced base theory. But, Millett does not return in detail to base defense during subsequent chapters. Advanced base defense and its culmination in the defense battalion are given cursory coverage. The Corps' amphibious assault role monopolizes Millett's space from the 1920s until after the Japanese attack on Pearl Harbor.

Other historians of the Marine Corps also downplay base defense in favor of amphibious assault as the Corps' mission most worthy of study.[11] On one level, this concentration is warranted because of the glorious role amphibious assault played in the Pacific War. But, on another level, overemphasis of amphibious assault excludes other essential areas of the Corps' long-term development.

Consequently, a historiographical void exists. A critical and analytical investigation of Holcomb and the defense battalion has not been written. Using recently declassified records, this thesis addresses two such neglected areas by establishing Thomas Holocmb as an important facilitator for the defense battalion, the Corps' "unique" and "single, great mission" until the late 1930s. In recent works, Nathan Prefer and Craig M. Cameron argue that the base defense was one of the Corps' primary missions—if the primary mission— from 1898 until the 1930s.[12] My research confirms and adds to their assertions by unearthing material from the National Archives and conducting surveys of Marine veterans of the 7th Defense Battalion.[13] Several other works also treat the base defense or Thomas Holcomb either directly or in part. These histories complement my research.[14]

PURPOSE AND SCOPE

Commandant Thomas Holcomb was an excellent strategist, manager, and publicist. Understanding his actions will help illuminate the mentality and institutions of the military and government prior to World War II. The defense battalion provides a case study for examining Holcomb's leadership. Defense battalions also clearly found their roots in long-standing advanced base defense theory.

As Commandant from 1936 to 1943, Holcomb directed the Corps' expansion including the creation of the heavily armed defense battalion. On a tactical level, planners designed these units to defend island outposts against air, sea, and amphibious assaults. Likewise, in holding island bases in the central and western Pacific, defense battalions fit into the grand strategy of the United States Navy. They comprised one half of the Corps' dual missions: amphibious assault and base defense. Finally, defense battalions served an equally pivotal public relations function as Holcomb struggled to market the Marine Corps as a vital and unique branch of the American military.

Serious challenges confronted Commandant Thomas Holcomb. For example, he was plagued by lack of funds, promotion stagnation, slow supply lines, and the isolationist tendencies of Congress and the American public. Throughout this study, the Corps' complete dependence on outside forces becomes abundantly clear. Sometimes Holcomb benefited from events beyond his control. Other times, he fought to turn seemingly damaging events into advantages for the Corps.

Chapter One traces the development of advanced base defense from theory in 1898 to reality in 1939 with the advent of the defense battalion. Before World War I, the Marine Corps struggled to present itself as fulfilling a particular mission: advanced base defense. During the 1920 and 1930s, the Corps barely survived isolationism's budgetary onslaught. But, with threat of the Japanese looming ever larger in the Pacific, Marines established their tactical and strategic dual mission: base defense and amphibious assault. The offensive gradually grew to overshadow the defensive. Upon promotion to Major General Commandant in 1936, the multi-talented Holcomb not only played politician and salesman but also oversaw strategy and tactics.

Chapter Two begins with the outbreak of hostilities in Europe in September of 1939. War in Europe awakened America's desire for preparedness and accelerated the rearmament program. However, low budgets continued to plague the Marines. In addition to strategy and tactics, the defense battalion increased its vital public relations role in the civil-military relationship. This involved not only reiterating the Corps' mission but also obtaining scarce resources. Once again, Holcomb played the roles of salesman and politician. But, he could accomplish very little without outside forces' assistance. With the successful reelection bid by President Franklin Delano Roosevelt in November 1940, the Corps' future brightened.

Chapter Three recounts the increasingly positive developments for the Corps in 1941. ABC-1 Talks and an upgrade to RAINBOW 5 firmly establish the Corps as the ideal base defense and amphibious assault force. As expansion accelerated, interservice rivalries for resources arose. Throughout 1941, Holcomb primarily faced administrative and bureaucratic challenges: obtaining a share of resources and guaranteeing that the resources were in the right place at the right time. These challenges triggered new managerial and logistical obstacles. An over-abundance of officers replaced the previous problem of stagnation in the officer corps. Difficulty in allocation and transportation of men and material replaced the former appropriation of men and equipment. Yet, despite Holcomb's efforts, the Marine Corps' full combat readiness remained largely fictional on the eve of the attack of Pearl Harbor.

CHAPTER 1

ADVANCED BASE THEORY TO REALITY, 1898-1939

INTRODUCTION

The United States Marine Corps' advanced base force originated in theory in 1898 and evolved into the defense battalion in 1938. Before World War I, the Corps had struggled to find a distinct purpose for existence. America's victory in the Spanish-American War had made advanced island bases became necessary to protect international interests. After World War I, strategists added an amphibious assault component to complement advanced base defense. The Corps presented itself as the logical choice for this dual defensive and offensive mission. However, the return to "normalcy" with its budget cuts and isolationist national strategy hampered the Corps' attempt to carve out its strategic niche. The Great Depression compounded the fiscal problems facing the Corps. Several events positively influenced the Corps' situation. First, in 1933, Franklin Roosevelt became President. With the assistance of several members of Congress, he raised the level of military preparedness. Second, in 1936, Roosevelt promoted Thomas Holcomb to Major General Commandant (MGC) of the Marine Corps. Uniquely gifted in administration and public relations, Holcomb ably led the Corps through its expansion from peace to war. Finally, when international tensions in the 1930s required a military buildup, the Corps moved to fulfill its dual mission of base defense and seizure. Advance base defense matured in 1939 with the advent of the defense battalion.[1]

SELLING BASE DEFENSE THEORY TO THE CORPS AND THE NAVY

Throughout its first 122 years of existence, the United States Marine Corps acted as constabulary security and seaborne soldiers. While America remained a continental power, those two missions remained sufficient for the Corps. The defeat of Spain in 1898 propelled America into the great power fraternity. This watershed event transformed both America's position in the world and the Corps' role in Naval strategy. Obtaining overseas possessions like the Philippines, Guam, and Wake increased overseas strategic and economic responsibilities. Hawaii ceased to be America's defensive frontier. A new defensive perimeter extended to the Philippines.[2]

The significance of an enlarged dominion was not lost on the General Board of the United States Navy. A larger fleet and a new Naval strategy were necessary to project American force over a larger area. Naval planners realized that the American fleet could dominate the seas only if bases existed from which to operate. To fulfill this strategic requirement, the Navy's General Board charged the Marine Corps with defending the outlying bases. Thus, the theory of advanced base defense was born.[3]

In 1902, Marine Captain Dion Williams published "The Defense of Our New Naval Stations" in *Proceedings of the United States Naval Institute*.[4] According to his article, the Corps' place in the new Naval strategy derived from Alfred Thayer Mahan's basic postulate: any war in which America might become involved would be—at least in its early stages—a naval conflict.[5] In his application of Mahanian strategy, Williams advocated utilizing islands like Guam and Samoa as safe harbors, coaling stations, repair facilities, and supply depots. Those island bases became known as "advanced bases."

Because the United States Navy would virtually monopolize the bases, Williams believed those bases "should be entirely controlled by the Navy, and not as in the case of the forts and shore stations of the continental territory, by the army."[6] Keeping the Corps subordinate to the Navy would alleviate the problem of unifying command between Navy and Army. Preaching to the skeptics among his fellow Marines, Williams proclaimed the Corps to be the obvious choice to defend the Navy's bases. Williams also believed that these expanded responsibilities justified an increase in the Corps and the Navy strengths.[7] Thus, he set the stage for further development of the theory of advanced base defense.

Because the Corps' strength stood at less than 10,000 men and officers between 1900 and 1910, many Marines viewed the base defense mission with little enthusiasm. Only a few innovative officers like Williams, Robert H. Dunlap, Eli K. Cole, John H. Russell, and John A. Lejeune showed any genuine interest in advanced base defense. With shortages of men and equipments, Commandant George F. Elliot remained reluctant to detach men from other more traditional duties on board ships and in American territories.[8]

ADVANCED BASE DEFENSE THEORY TAKES SHAPE

During the first decade of the new century, advanced base defense made some progress toward acceptance. For example, Dion Williams outlined a plan in 1907 to organize both fixed and mobile defense forces. Little more than planning had yet resulted. In 1910, a turning point in the development of advanced base defense occurred. At the direction of the Navy Department and the General Board, newly appointed Commandant William P. Biddle founded the Advanced Base School. In this program, Marines explored issues like artillery placement, communications, logistics, and staff organization. The school prepared its students for maneuvers, the goal of their peace-time education. With proper training and equipment, the General Board believed that Marines would effectively fulfill the base defense mission.[9]

In 1914, drawing-board theories came of age in a simulated attack against Culebra, a small island in the Caribbean. Elements of the United States Atlantic Fleet attacked 1,723 Marines defending the island. The Marine Advanced Base Brigade succeeded beyond expectations. Moreover, "in an extraordinarily efficient manner," this unit quickly fortified the island, harassed the attacking flotilla, and repulsed amphibious assaults. The Advanced Base Brigade lasted as a unit until 1919. Significant for the long-term development of the Corps as well as advanced base defense, three future Marine Corps Commandants—George Barnett, John A. Lejeune, and Wendell C. Neville—received practical field experience at Culebra.[10]

Beyond the tactical lessons of fire control and reserve placement learned at Culebra, Naval planners also explored strategic issues in several significant reports written under the auspices of the Naval War College. According to one study written in 1913, possible adversaries in a Pacific war included Germany, Japan, or Great Britain. Japan's victory in the Russo-Japanese War in 1905 placed it as the dominant power in the western Pacific. Because of a deficiency in natural resources, Japan jealously eyed the resource-rich Asian mainland. Thus, any southward or westward expansion would inevitably bring Japan into direct conflict with America's expanding strategic and commercial interests in the area. American security dictated the need for a strong Naval presence and its corollary of safe Naval bases.[11]

Guam was the archetype for a potential advanced base. Strategically, this island formed the hub of a wheel with trading routes and communication lines as the spokes. From a base on Guam, the United States "fleet would bear on every point from Singapore to Vladivostok." Naval strategists conceded that units on Guam would likely face Japan's local military superiority. Yet, despite its acknowledged theoretical importance, Guam remained vulnerable to potential attack as of 1913.[12]

By 1915, the Marine Corps was recognized as ideal advanced base force. A Naval War College report offered two conclusions that specifically placed the Corps and advanced base defense in their strategic contexts:

> (a) In the event of war, particularly with a Naval power, it will be necessary for the fleet to have with it, or at its disposal, a force properly equipped and capable of seizing and holding one or more temporary bases in advance of its permanent bases; and

> (b) The Marine Corps, in view of this training and relation to the Navy, is the force best suited to perform such work.[13]

Once again, while the Navy's acknowledgement of the Corps as "the force best suited to perform" base defense was a victory, neither the Navy nor the civilian government allocated the resources to make base defense a reality.

WORLD WAR I'S IMPACT ON THE CORPS AND BASE DEFENSE

From the Corps' internal perspective, the war in Europe affected base defense theory in several tangential, yet significant, ways. Involvement in the conflict strengthened America's military in general and the Corps in particular. Civilian leadership heeded previous recommendations for more men and better matériel. The Corps greatly benefited from heightened American preparedness in at least two ways: an increase in manpower to one-fifth of Naval manpower and increases in appropriations for the development, training, and maintenance of advanced base forces.[14]

Marine involvement in World War I represented a departure from its usual duties as constabulary and shipboard security. As part of the American Expeditionary Force, Marines served as infantry in the trenches of France. While trench warfare did not directly affect advance base theory, Marines still gained valuable combat experience. For example, many of the Corps' future leaders like Thomas Holcomb won their spurs in the trenches. In addition, courageous Marine exploits in battles like Belleau Wood and Chateau-Thierry made for good publicity. To describe battle-hardened veterans, nicknames like "devil dogs" and the "old breed" emerged in Marine lore. Participation in World War I also helped consolidate important features like the Marine Corps Reserves, Women Marines, and Marine Aviation.[15]

World War I intensified potential antagonism between the United States and Japan. The European powers had focused all their resources on the continent and did not give sufficient attention to the Far East. As a result, Japan was left with a relatively free hand in the region. Japan obtained Germany's Pacific possessions as part of the Treaty of Versailles. Consequently, the stage was set for future conflict between Japan and America.[16]

Because the United States emerged from the war as the premier world power, American strategic and commercial interests around the world increased. These interests required a strong military for protection. For example, advanced base defense constituted a major part of Naval strategy in the Pacific. In 1919, strategic planning for the use of advanced bases was enlarged to include the logistical support for submarines, another offensive weapon. Bases, submarines, and a fleet in the Pacific implied preparation for a potential conflict with Japan. With an offensive war in mind, Naval planners needed Marine units both to defend American bases and seize Japanese bases. Thus, an amphibious component grew in significance. Once again, the Corps promoted itself as the logical choice for both halves of the mission: defense and seizure.[17]

In 1920, John A. Lejeune became the Commandant of the Marine Corps. He envisioned a Corps that would defend and seize bases. But, in his nine-year tenure as Commandant, Lejeune faced numerous challenges resulting from lower budgets in America's return to normalcy. Internally, he introduced several reforms like establishing a board to oversee the promotion process and reorganizing the Marine Corps Schools. The new promotion procedure gave Lejeune "an officer corps balanced between proven troop leaders and staff specialists." Moreover, the reorganized Marine Corps Schools "gave the Commandant an important vehicle for propelling his officers to new professional heights and indoctrinating them in Headquarters policy." Both these reforms also helped maintain *esprit de corps* among commissioned and enlisted personnel. Lejeune's reforms did not succeed entirely. During the interwar years, an officer could expect to retire after thirty years as a senior captain or junior major. Promotion stagnation made high morale difficult to maintain. For all the setbacks, future Marine generals like Thomas Holcomb, Alexander Vandegrift, and Holland Smith flourished under Lejeune's leadership.[18]

During Lejeune's Commandancy, the Corps attempted to solidify its place in American strategy. To help accomplish this task, Marine Major Earl H. Ellis published the two definitive works on bases and Pacific Naval strategy in 1921. His Navy Bases: Their Location, Resources, and Security and Advanced Base Operations in Micronesia expanded on previous studies for the Naval War College. These two reports served as the foundation for the eventual development of the Fleet Marine Force in 1933. Moreover, Ellis prophesied the importance of advanced base operations in the World War II.[19]

In *Navy Bases*, Ellis reasserted the significance of outposts in supporting the fleet. Before World War I, guaranteeing the Monroe Doctrine had required merely defending the hemisphere. With greater strategic and economic considerations in the 1920s, insurance of the Open Door Policy in the Far East consisted of offensive and defensive objectives. Ellis believed that successful maintenance of outlying bases insured a successful Naval campaign.[20]

Because of its "power and position" as "the only purely Pacific world power," Ellis pointed to Japan as America's principal adversary in the Pacific. He accurately predicted that Japan would take the offensive and attempt to capture America's outlying bases. Therefore, the Japanese would build a buffer zone for themselves. In his recommendations, Ellis identified the Marine Corps, since it was a component of the Navy, as the best force to seize and defend advanced bases. This assertion represented a consistent and continuous attempt by the Corps to market itself with a significant purpose.[21]

Ellis' *Advanced Base Operations in Micronesia* served as a companion work to *Naval Bases*. *Operations* outlined a strategy for seizure and defense of islands in the Pacific including the Japanese-held Marianas, Marshall, and Caroline island chains. Imagining a potential campaign in the Pacific, Ellis discussed the probable amphibious assaults and surface battles. From America's strategic perspective, these maneuvers commenced with the capture of the Marshall Islands and climaxed with the seizure of the Palau Islands. The Japanese fleet would also be met and decisively defeated. As the Marines captured bases, these same bases must be held against potential counterattack. Consequently, training for both seizure and defense should take place simultaneously.[22]

Ellis' evaluation of Pacific strategy became even more crucial because of the 1922 Five Power Treaty. This agreement among the great powers compounded America's strategic disadvantage in the western Pacific by setting a ratio of 5:5:3 for American, British, and Japanese capital ship tonnage. Whereas Japan needed to safeguard only one ocean, the United States and Britain needed to safeguard three. To make matters worse, the Five Power Treaty prohibited the United States from fortifying bases in the western Pacific; bases in the central Pacific and eastern Indian Ocean had to suffice. Upholding the Open Door and protecting American territories justified a strong Corps: "a mobile force to accompany the Fleet for operations on shore in support of the Fleet."[23] Consequently, the Corps found itself firmly ensconced in its strategic niche: both seizure and defense of bases in the Pacific. Although the Five Power Treaty limited the size of capital ships and placement of Naval bases, it did not limit support to auxiliary units like Marine advanced base defense forces.

In a pair of 1923 articles in Marine Corps Gazette, Commandant John Lejeune and Marine General Rufus Lane restated Ellis' argument: seizing and defending advanced bases was paramount to success in war. Like previous Naval writers, both Lejeune and Lane appealed to the Mahanian theory of Naval strategy: a strong ocean-going fleet enabled a nation to project military force on a global scale. In a potential war with Japan, "control of the Pacific was essential in order to defeat Japan … there is no question that without victory at sea there would be no victory on land or in the air." However, achieving supremacy in the Pacific posed a major obstacle for the Navy and the Marine Corps. The Navy had to project military force in the East Asian region despite the overwhelming local advantage enjoyed by the Japanese. Although base seizure had played a secondary role in earlier Naval strategy, it increased in significance because of the Five Power Treaty of 1922.[24] Both Lejeune and Lane explicitly attempted to sell the Marine Corps as the ideal force to support the United States Navy in a future conflict.

Marketing the Corps and obtaining the necessary resources to fulfill its mission became the next goal. To accomplish this, Lejeune attempted to improve relations with Congress, the Presidency, and the American public.[25] Yet, despite efforts by and on behalf of the Corps, reductions in force persisted during the 1920s and 1930s. After World War I, the American public's interest in the military waned. Frugality was the watchword. In 1922, a suggested strength of 27,000 Marines would enable the Corps to meet "peace-time requirements, and make possible some preparations for the future." But a civilian administration and public wishing for a return to normalcy rejected the suggestion and even lowered Marine manpower from 21,000 in 1922 to 19,000 in 1926. Promotion stagnation compounded the manpower deficiencies. Moreover, difficulties in rewarding worthy officers with rank advancement made retention of these same officers problematic.[26]

Although severe shortages existed, the dark cloud of budget cuts did have its silver lining. As aide to Commandant John H. Russell from 1934 to 1936, Charles F. Good observed that every Marine received various assignments and developed multiple skills. Furthermore, because of the Corps' small size, a natural cross-training and flexibility resulted. For example, the "overhead people, like the mess force and administrative people, all had battle stations." When expansion did occur in the late 1930s, the Corps was better prepared to make a relatively smooth transition.[27]

THE "ORANGE" PLAN AND ITS SIGNIFICANCE FOR THE CORPS

Because of the difficulties inherent in meeting the Japanese threat, American military strategists formulated a series of contingencies called the ORANGE Plan. The 1926 ORANGE Plan envisioned "an offensive war, primarily Naval, directed toward the isolation and exhaustion of Japan, through offensive operations against her Naval forces and economic life."[28] According to military historian Edward S. Miller, younger Naval strategists or "cautionaries" gradually concluded that a long war of attrition would be necessary to defeat Japan.[29]

Hypothetically, while the Army and the Marine Corps held the Philippines and other Pacific bases, the American fleet would fight its way across the Pacific. The Japanese Navy would be engaged and defeated in a decisive battle. Simultaneously, the Japanese would be deprived of their island bases and eventually forced into capitulation. In *Rising Sun in the Pacific*, military historian Samuel Eliot Morison underscores the necessity of island bases in the ORANGE Plan. The Navy's strategists saw Midway and Wake as excellent bases for patrol planes and submarines. In addition, Guam served as a key point for the Pacific conflict. Morrison bluntly states that Guam "would be of tremendous assistance in this defensive phase of the war ...." It could be used as supply depot and a forward base to neutralize Saipan.[30]

The interservice report Joint Action of the Army and Navy (1926) summarized the mission and purpose of the Marine Corps within the ORANGE plan's grand strategy.[31] The Departments of War and the Navy designated several duties. These entailed the provision and maintenance of forces:

(a) For land operations in support of the fleet for the initial seizure and defense of advanced bases and for such limited auxiliary land operations as are essential to the prosecution of the Naval campaign.

(b) For emergency service in time of peace for the protection of the interests of the United States in foreign countries.

(c) For Marine detachments on vessels of the fleet and for interior protection of Naval shore stations.[32]

Of these, the first was "fundamental." The constant argument for Naval bases did bear fruit because the ORANGE Plan contained "a new mandate for the Corps." Toward this end, the Marine Corps carved out its niche: dual missions of amphibious assault and island defense.[33] However, theory did not intersect with reality; the Corps' significance in strategy did not translate into increases in Marine appropriations, equipment, and manpower.

THE GREAT DEPRESSION

The stock market crash of 1929 precipitated an even greater military downsizing. Budget cuts intensified the financial woes plaguing the Marine Corps. The Federal Government—goaded by an economy-minded and isolationist public—slashed the personnel in the Marine Corps and the Navy. From 1931 until 1934, the Corps received a 24.4 percent reduction and the Navy a 5.6 percent reduction. The budgetary onslaught occurred on at least two levels. Political scientist Samuel Huntington labels one level of attackers as "business pacifists;" this group saw a military buildup as a misuse of resources which could have been more wisely spent elsewhere. The other level of attackers could be called the "anti-business-military partnership;" this group believed the military buildup was merely an outlet for over-production.[34]

During this dark period, Commandant Wendell C. Neville continued to strengthen the Corps' status as a seaborne military force. He proclaimed the Corps to be "versatile in the extreme." Justifying this statement, he explained the Corps furnished the Navy with units capable of both land and sea duty. Neville also outlined the Corps' educational system. Marines attended the Army Artillery School, Motor Transportation School, Signal Corps School, Flight School, the War Colleges, and the Command and General Staff Schools. This helped establish professionalism and maintain *esprit de corps* among commissioned and enlisted personnel.[35]

However, not all Neville's insights were so positive. For example, He felt that Marines needed to be individuals with great motivation and dedication. Neville observed that "a discontented man, or an ambitious man who sees nothing ahead, does not re-enlist. Pay, living conditions and opportunities for advancement have a direct relation to efficiency and morale." Stagnation of promotions and low pay remained a serious problem, which only budget increases could alleviate.[36]

The Navy also consistently promoted the Corps as the premier seaborne support force. According to Lieutenant Commander E. W. Broadbent in 1931, the Corps essentially operated as the United States Navy's private army. He asked and answered two rhetorical questions in the following: "Why should the Navy maintain its own army? What does it do with this army? The answer to these question lies almost entirely in one word 'bases.'"[37] This statement mirrored the Marines' own rhetoric. Broadbent even quoted Lejeune's 1923 article verbatim. Both authors considered the Corps' mission to be "vital to the successful operation of the fleet in war." Although Broadbent concentrated on the amphibious assault, his article clearly showed the Marine Corps' importance for defensive and offensive operations in Navy strategy.[38]

On a purely functional level, the Navy also utilized the Corps as a deterrent to the Army's interference in the Pacific. The Navy justified this action because the Army proved inadequate for the base defense mission. First, Army units lacked the necessary training in amphibious warfare and seamanship. Second, tanks, heavy artillery, and large supply trains encumbered the Army. Conversely, Marine units possessed mobile yet potent weapons like the 75 mm pack howitzer. Third, the Army's strategists did not support the Naval emphasis in the ORANGE Plan because they believed it was unwise, expensive, and inglorious for the Army. Furthermore, the ORANGE Plan placed the Philippines in a vulnerable position and expected Army units to hold it for as long as six months.[39] Finally, unity of command was absolutely crucial to the success of any mission—especially an amphibious assault. Fire control aboard the support ships must be carefully coordinated with close air support and landing operations. With the Marine Corps as a component of the Navy, problems of Army-Navy cooperation or competition might hopefully be avoided.[40] The Joint Board of the Army and Navy ideally should have coordinated joint operations between the two branches. However, before the Second World War, lack of communication made any such cooperation problematic.[41]

In addition, national priorities were neither established nor followed. On the international scene, a clear foreign and military policy was needed. The situation in the Far East grew increasingly ominous because of the Japanese occupation of Manchuria in 1931. A constant thirst for the natural resources of China heightened Japanese ambitions. Yet, the Hoover Administration's decidedly domestic focus failed to formulate a consistent policy in the Far East.[42]

Faced with fiscal obstacles, the Corps continued to develop within the strategic framework of assault and defense of advanced bases. While fortification plans for Wake, Palmyra, Guam, Midway, and other Pacific islands began in the early 1930s, base construction and maneuvers slowed to a standstill because the Federal government concentrated on a domestic agenda.[43]

Without coherent guidance in foreign policy from the civilian government, the armed services attempted to unravel American objectives by themselves. The military, as a whole, perceived national strategy as defensive. The United States Army was ill prepared for any conflict, defensive or otherwise. For their part, the Navy's strategists saw a twofold mission: first, defend American possessions and interests in the Far East; and, second, safeguard the Monroe Doctrine in the Western Hemisphere.[44]

Military strategists' conclusions led to more tenuous preparation for nonexistent goals. Confusion arose because the American tendency toward isolationism ignored an increasingly tense international situation. Contemporary Marines also drew similar conclusions regarding strategy and civil-military relations. From his perspective as Military Secretary to the MGC during the late 1930s, a critical Alexander Vandegrift concluded that the military failed to specify exact threats. Moreover, he indicted a number of groups in the following:

This was the job of the State Department, the Army and the Navy—each of which almost totally neglected it. In turn the true significance of vital international issues escaped in whole or in part officers of the armed forces, members of Congress, and the bulk of the American people.[45]

Consequently, any efficient civil-military harmony was limited, if not negligible. If this absence of communication was not bad enough, the military's infrastructure could not follow a well-defined strategy even if one had existed.

EFFECTS OF THE 1932 ELECTION ON THE CORPS

The Corps had languished under the Hoover Administration from 1929 through 1932. But in the election of 1932, Franklin Roosevelt ascended to the Presidency. Having served as Assistant Secretary of the Navy during the First World War, President Roosevelt looked sympathetically on the Navy and the Marine Corps' plight. He favored and supported both seaborne services. Roosevelt's election to the Presidency "came as a relief to the Navy." In a letter to the newly elected President, Chief of Naval Operations (CNO) William V. Pratt conveyed the general satisfaction within the Navy in the following: "a pleasure ... to know that the fate of the Navy lies in the hands of a man who so loves it as you do."[46] Historian Lester H. Brune asserted that President Roosevelt eventually "became the necessary catalyst, uniting previously uncoordinated military and diplomatic actions and seeking a unified national security strategy." Brune's position is similar to most historians' positions.[47]

In the framework of American civil-military relations, the executive branch supervised the "external" or "operational" aspects of the military. The major question was "how" to use the military. Thus, the executive branch specifically dealt with the following areas: "number and type of ships, the number and status of personnel, the extent and location of the shore establishment, and the administration of the Navy Department."[48] For advice in these matters, President Roosevelt increasingly relied on the military staffs rather than his civilian staffs in the War and Navy Departments. He enjoyed "very close and direct working relationships with" military leaders like CNO Harold Stark and Army Chief of Staff (COS) George Marshall. The military's task included generating contingency plans and coordinating these plans with national objectives. For his part in the civil-military relationship, Roosevelt increasingly presented "the armed forces with unprecedented direction, guidance, and coordination." Thus, he circumvented the State, Navy, and War Departments and partially displaced Congress. Military advisors were at least on par with the diplomatic and political advisors to the President. Relative coordination and even cooperation existed between the Presidency and the military. However, competition and rivalry persisted among the armed services.[49]

The Navy and the Marine Corps also gained powerful allies in Congress because of the 1932 elections. Representative Carl Vinson (D-GA) assumed the influential chairmanship of the House Naval Affairs Committee. In this capacity, "Uncle Carl" acted as patron saint for both seaborne services. As a self-proclaimed "big Navy man" like Roosevelt, he provided instrumental support in passing the 1934 and 1938 Naval Appropriation Bills and thus promoted expansion of the Navy and Marine Corps. The following epitaph showed Vinson's significance during the dark days of the Depression: "It is evident, that without the staunch and unwavering persistence of this farsighted Georgian, the United States Navy would have been far worse off that it was in December of 1941 ...."[50]

In addition to Vinson, Representative Melvin Maas (R-MN) also proved instrumental in expanding the Corps. In his role as ranking Republican on the House Naval Affairs Committee, he worked closely with Vinson to sponsor legislation to fortify Guam and institute reforms in the Navy's promotion system. Maas personally embodied civil-military relations as both Member of Congress (1925-1933 and 1935-1945) and Lieutenant Colonel in the Marine Corps Reserve.[51]

Despite the presence of military advocates in the White House and Congress, increases in defense spending were neither guaranteed nor punctual. In acquiring appropriations in the late 1930s, the Marine Corps and the Navy constantly competed not only with a close-fisted public but also with the Army and its COS George Marshall for limited resources. During the above-mentioned 1931-1934 manpower reductions in the Navy and the Marine Corps, the Army suffered no reduction in personnel. Marshall did not always like the Marine Corps; at times, he was a "bitter rival." For example, although the Army may have won the struggle for manpower, Marshall quipped in 1933 that the Corps consistently seemed to possess better clothing than the Army. Furthermore, Marshall thought that Marines "have more money, because they are popular with Congress, and I believe they are less rigidly held to account for details of their expenditures ...." Whereas the rivalry between the military services hindered efficient cooperation, the competition did have the virtue of forcing each branch to concentrate on a particular task.[52]

FORMATION OF THE FLEET MARINE FORCE

In 1933, the ongoing effort to implement a more structured purpose in the Marine Corps culminated in the creation of the Fleet Marine Force (FMF). Initially, two small units at Quantico and San Diego comprised the whole FMF. The new name replaced the previous Marine Expeditionary Force. This former title carried a pair of negative connotations: first, it sounded too much like an interventionist unit, as it had functioned in the First World War; and, second, the former title of Marine Expeditionary Force too broadly described the narrowly defined roles of seizure and defense of bases. According to Commandant John Russell, the Marine Corps "should have a striking force, well equipped, well armed and highly trained, working as a unit of the Fleet under the direct orders of the Commander-in-Chief." The FMF fulfilled these criteria and thus formed an instrument to integrate the Corps into the Naval strategy. In addition, interservice, administrative, and command mechanisms were also established.[53] According to future member of the 1st Defense Battalion William J. Van Ryzin, the FMF's early days were primarily concerned with defense. Effective public relations prescribed a defensive vocabulary to appeal to isolationist tendencies of the American public.[54]

As the 1930s progressed, the military's strategists risked bad publicity by shifting moving from a purely defensive emphasis to a combination of offensive and defensive emphases. Despite the Britain's amphibious fiasco at Gallipoli in World War I, Marine and Naval tacticians believed ship-to-shore assaults were feasible. Through meticulous planning, the tactical advantages retained by defenders could be and were overcome. Lessons were thus learned from Gallipoli. The key to a successful amphibious landing was the principle of combined arms: "only the Marine Corps with a narrowly defined mission ... appears to have emphasized a balanced, all-arms approach to combat."[55] Planners covered six areas: command relations, Naval gun support, aerial support, ship-to-movement, securing the beachhead, and logistics. Moreover, during landing exercises, mutually beneficial lessons could be learned by both the assaulting and the assaulted Marines. In sum, the FMF "provided the Navy with a 'type-force' of reinforced infantry with the specific mission of executing landing operations."[56]

In 1934, the Marine Corps compiled the *Tentative Manual of Landing Operations* for the Navy. This handbook of amphibious operations displayed the classic example of the Corps' appreciation for all aspects of strategy and tactics. In summarizing all the previous work of Navy and Marine Corps planners, the *Tentative Manual* solidified the Corps' duty to support Naval operations "by land operations in the seizure, defense, and holding of temporary advanced bases ...." The *Tentative Manual* subsequently equated the term "temporary advanced base" with "a Naval base of temporary nature" and "an advanced base." A base's transitory importance in a Naval campaign made it relevant to the Corps' mission.[57]

Naval strategy and tactics placed a premium on the mobility of the FMF. In contrast, the Army guarded bases of a more permanent nature or relieved Marines for more activities directly supporting the fleet. Ironically, neither the Army nor the Navy wanted to allocate their own resources for such a specialized assignment. This resulted in the Corps' isolation and insulation; Marines used their monopoly on advance base operations to develop unique tactics.[58]

HOLCOMB'S APPOINTMENT AS MAJOR GENERAL COMMANDANT

Despite all the Corps' posturing, the Great Depression's low defense budgets lingered. Marines still used equipment from the First World War and overstretched their limited manpower. In addition, the Corps faced other problems: promotion bottlenecks, low morale, interservice rivalries, and Congress's budgetary restraints.[59] At the low point in this quagmire, Thomas Holcomb assumed the rank of MGC of the Marine Corps in December of 1936.

Holcomb's background and experiences in the Corps for over thirty-five years prepared him for his command responsibilities. He was born in 1879 and began his career in the Corps as a second lieutenant in April 1900. Although Holcomb was not a graduate of the Naval Academy, he served with distinction in a variety of assignments from China to the Philippines. He also launched the Marine Corps Rifle Team and competed on the team at the National Matches, winning the national championship in 1911. During the First World War, Holcomb broadened his experience as commanding officer of the 2nd Battalion, 6th Marines in the Army Expeditionary Force. His leadership at the Battle of Belleau Wood won him decorations and promotions. Eventually, he joined the staff of the Army's 2nd Division. Holcomb's stint in France afforded invaluable training in administration as well as combat leadership. He even attracted the attention of soon-to-be Commandant John A. Lejeune.

Under Lejeune's direction, Holcomb distinguished himself at the Army and Navy War Colleges. With education and experience behind him, Holcomb eventually became the head of the Marine Corps Schools at Quantico, Virginia in early 1935. Under his direction, base defense and amphibious assault theories matured. Holcomb impressed then-incumbent Commandant John H. Russell enough to be promoted over more senior officers for the next Commandancy.[60]

Serving as MGC until 1943, Holcomb played the pivotal role in the growth of the Corps as strategist, administrator, and publicist. His fellow Marines, the Navy, the Congress, and the White House respected him. While serving as Holcomb's aide from 1937 to 1940, Robert H. Williams saw Holcomb as a "plain spoken" and "very alert" leader. Moreover, his leadership "inspire[d] confidence and trust and a belief in his judgement …." Williams' praise was indicative of a seemingly universal admiration for Holcomb from the highest-ranking officer to the lowliest enlisted man.[61] Marines serving in the lower ranks made similar observations: Holcomb "was the father of the modern Marine Corps," "was a good General," "held the Corps together," "tried his best to enlarge the Corps," and "was a damn good salesman."[62]

Holcomb performed several indispensable jobs during his Commandancy: administrator supervising the increasing size of the Corps, strategist perfecting the Corps' amphibious assault techniques, and salesman cajoling the civilian government into supporting the Corps. During his first two years of command, Thomas Holcomb concentrated on relations with the public and Congress. Both were essential reforming the Marine Corps because it was almost totally dependent on external patrons for existence. Public support provided the best avenue to gaining financial support from Congress.[63]

RELATIONS WITH THE PUBLIC AND CONGRESS

The Corps developed a impressive public relations machine. Like his predecessors, Holcomb constantly attempted to bolster the image of "the Leathernecks as America's paramount fighting force" in the eyes of the American public and their Congressional representatives. In a letter to Alexander Vandegrift, Charles Lyman summarized the value of good self-promotion for the Corps: "Friendships must be built up with the other branches of the service, with Congress, and with civilians who enjoy an influential status, if we are going to secure essentials and cease to be a `shoe string' organization." Following this postulate, Holcomb used his position as a platform to promote the Corps' missions and the need for men and matériel to complete these missions. Publicity came in many forms: radio broadcasts, motion pictures, Civil War battle reenactments, public addresses, and periodical articles.[64]

Almost immediately upon assuming command of the Corps, Thomas Holcomb launched his publicity campaign. A 1937 speech to the Women's Patriotic Conference on National Defense exemplified his pro-Corps rhetoric. Holcomb began by reflecting on global turmoil: "mankind is ruled no longer by law but by man. Government is by decree and fiat." In this unpredictable world, the United States of America stood as a "bulwark" of order and civility. From this introduction, Holcomb presented the Marine Corps as an integral element of America's first line of defense. Specifically, he identified the seizure and defense of island bases as "axiomatic" and "vital" to Naval success in a Pacific conflict. Holcomb's assertion was not new; he had merely reiterated Mahan's ingrained Naval postulate. In his conclusion, Holcomb called for increased financial support for the

Corps. Although he clearly pointed to a defensive mode, particularly for the FMF, he also skillfully suggested an offensive amphibious mandate.[65]

Beyond courting public opinion, Thomas Holcomb also initiated better relations with Congress. He devoted significant energy to encourage passage of bills which benefitted the Corps; he even enlisted retired Marines like John A. Lejeune to help lobby Congress. Specific items to be covered in appropriations bills included ration allowances, small arms ammunition, automobiles, and war reserve ammunition. In 1937, Holcomb believed that the Corps won a victory when the money appropriated for these items was reduced rather than deleted from that year's bill.[66]

The 1938 Naval Personnel Bill served as a prime example—albeit largely unsuccessful— of Holcomb's lobbying efforts. This legislation called for improvements in the Marine Corps. Long-standing problems had existed regarding promotion schedules, so this bill called for a reform of the promotion system. On the top end of the ranks, general officers were limited to serving seven years at their current grade and allowed only two reviews for promotion before retirement. This measure would presumably expedite advancement in rank. The 1938 bill also entailed raising Corps strength to one-fifth of Naval strength, raising the percentage of privates first class from 25 to 40 percent, and raising the officers to enlisted men ratio from 4.5 to 5.5 percent. Aside from the "decided improvement" of calling for increased manpower, the 1938 personnel bill failed to appropriate the necessary funds to raise manpower.[67]

Before passage, the 1938 Naval Personnel Bill had been deleted from the 1938 Naval Expansion Bill. Representative Carl Vinson pushed the Naval Expansion Bill through Congress in May of that year. It authorized an increase in capital ship tonnage. Of course, it was noteworthy that the Japanese occupation of China succeeded in awakening Congress out of its budgetary stupor. As for relevance to the Corps, the 1938 Naval Expansion Bill called for strengthening or the establishment of Naval bases in American territories. Thus, the Corps stood to benefit from the expansion. However, the base expansion proposal was also stricken from the final legislation in spite of Vinson's patronage. Those opposing Vinson, particularly Republican Representatives like Hamilton Fish and Frank Church, believed that reinforcing Guam would provoke the already militant Japanese rather than discourage them. While Holcomb and his Congressional patrons did not always improve the Corps' level of preparedness, they certainly stemmed the tide of ever-decreasing appropriations, which had troubled the Corps for fifteen years.[68]

CULMINATION OF BASE DEFENSE THEORY: THE DEFENSE BATTALION

In opposition to dissenting Congressmen, the final report of the Navy's Hepburn Board endorsed the fortification of Pacific Naval bases—especially Guam but also Midway, Palmyra, Johnston, and Wake—in their report of December 1938. Specifically, the Hepburn Board recommended that these outposts be fully developed and equipped for use by submarines, aircraft, and surface vessels. Because Naval and Marine strategists had constantly preached this message since the turn of the century, the recommendation was not innovative. The recommendation was indeed more urgent than ever in light of Japanese aggression in China and the German threat in Europe.

Members of the Hepburn Board contended that fortifications on western Pacific bases were strategic imperatives. Furthermore, these officers firmly believed that this deterred Japanese expansion against the Philippines, Southeast Asia, Midway, and even Hawaii. Agreement on this deterrent effect was not limited to the military. Stanley Hornbeck, a Far East expert in the State Department during the 1930s, saw the presence of United States forces in the Western Pacific as having "done much to prevent an open conflict with Japan." Whether deterrent or not, bases on the western Pacific islands had nothing resembling fortifications. Consequently, the Hepburn Board's edict generated interest in fortifying and supplying these outlying bases.[69]

The escalation of global tensions also prompted a greater desire for a strong defense of American strategic and economic interests. As a result of the ominous international situation, military strategists replaced the ORANGE Plan with the RAINBOW Plans. The new contingency plans designated Marine Corps "defense detachments" to be organized and stationed on Wake, Palmyra, Johnston, and Midway.[70] The potential threat from both Japan and Germany caused a complete overload of already limited military resources. Because restricted capabilities allowed only restricted goals, military strategists formulated the RAINBOW Plans in early 1939. This series of contingency plans amended the ORANGE Plan to allow for a war against Germany, Italy, and Japan under a variety of circumstances.

RAINBOW's most basic priority assumed hemispheric protection and, in the case of war, concentration on victory in Europe. This emphasis relegated outlying possessions like the Philippines and Western Pacific islands to defensive nature at best and marginalized them at worst.[71] On one level, the shift from the ORANGE to the "RAINBOW Plans did not appreciably alter the Marine Corps' role in strategic planning." Its mission still encompassed two goals: defense of advanced bases and assault against enemy bases. But, on another level, the Corps' theoretical role shifted back toward a defensive accent because battle schedules did not prescribe when an offensive would commence in the Pacific.[72]

In accordance with the Hepburn Board's recommendations, advanced base defense theory culminated in 1939 with the advent of Marine defense battalions, "up-to-date versions of the technical regiment in the old Advance Base Force." The units played "static defense" roles by "sacrificing tactical maneuverability for strategic mobility." Composed of about one thousand heavily-armed leathernecks, a defense battalion's sole purpose consisted of securing an island base in the face of enemy air, sea, and land attack. Although "modest" in manpower, a defense battalion boasted impressive firepower: twelve 3-inch anti-aircraft (AA) guns, forty-eight .50 caliber AA guns, forty-eight .30 caliber AA guns, and 6 Navy 5-inch guns. Defense battalions upgraded the usual Marine light infantry unit to a combination of an artillery and a heavy infantry unit. Strategically, these units had the virtue of rapid deployment and self-sufficiency. Thus, they were a "logical outgrowth" of Naval strategy and the Corps' mission.[73]

Thomas Holcomb and Marine Brigadier General Charles Barrett created the defense battalion to perform the Corps' defensive duties in RAINBOW. Lower ranking Marines also provide evidence of the connection between Holcomb and defense battalions. According to a 7th Defense Battalion Marine, Robert F. Cyperski, Holcomb "saw the need for first line defense before war." Furthermore, Salvatore J. Butta of the 7th believed

Holcomb "was very gung-ho about [defense battalions] in the Pacific area." Perhaps Antonio Santaniell of the 7th best summarizes Commandant Holcomb's role: he "was a strong advocate of defense battalions. He fought to get more men and equipment, especially in the beginning of the war."[74]

CONCLUSION

Although advanced base defense theory and Naval strategy coalesced in the defense battalion, the practical formation of any units exceeded available resources. The Corps had established itself as the ideal base defense and amphibious assault force. Naval strategists had also championed the Corps as the ideal seaborne force. The Roosevelt Administration even recognized the consequences of maintaining military readiness in general and Marine-held Pacific bases in particular. However, the practical problem of inadequate men and matériel remained a constant. Thomas Holcomb and the Marine Corps only partially achieved the goal of a genuine defense force. Circumstances beyond Holcomb's control would have to raise the fortunes of the Marine Corps and the defense battalion. German and Japanese hostility and hence American reaction would have to draw ever closer to motivate Congressional funding of the military. Meanwhile, the Corps continued its struggle for a share in the limited resources. Likewise, Thomas Holcomb's methodology continued to stress the Marine Corps defense battalion's unique capability as a base defense force. Less conspicuously, he also further enlarged the role of amphibious assault.

CHAPTER 2

THE TURNING POINT, 1939-1940

INTRODUCTION

This second chapter examines Commandant Thomas Holcomb's role in the ongoing development of the defense battalion during 1939 and 1940. The changing international, interservice, and the internal Corps contexts helped shape Holcomb's efforts to achieve preparedness. The increasingly strained international situation rendered the ORANGE Plan obsolete. The new, more flexible RAINBOW Plans replaced ORANGE. In the updated contingency plans, the Corps' dual missions of base defense and amphibious assault became more significant. Interservice rivalries intensified as Holcomb competed with a resource-hungry Army for attention from an isolationist public and Congress. Internally, numerous difficulties plagued the Corps. For example, meager resources had to be divided between the offensive mandate of amphibious assault and the defensive mandate of advanced bases. In these contexts, the defense battalion was a boon for the Corps: it provided a valuable tool for public relations, enabled the Corps to obtain more resources, and fulfilled an essential strategic function. However, the defense battalions also drained valuable men and matériel from other areas. In both external and internal matters, Holcomb's leadership played crucial roles in the Corps' move toward preparedness. Ultimately, the election of 1940 empowered Congress and President Roosevelt to raise America's military preparedness.

FRUGALITY IN THE CORPS DURING THE 1930S

Because of the spartan budgets of the 1930s, the American military suffered. A chorus of historians observe the military's impotence prior to the Second World War. Military historian Maurice Matloff bluntly summarizes their observations, "Twenty lean years had their effect, and by 1939, the armed forces were in no condition to conduct major military operations of the type required in the world-wide conflict ...." Although threats multiplied in Europe and the Pacific, an isolationist political environment hampered efforts to rearm. Appropriations, manpower, and the quantity and quality of weapons slumped. In short, "preparedness went down by default."[1]

These "lean years" compounded problems for the Corps. When serving as Military Secretary and later as Assistant to the MGC in 1940, Brigadier General Alexander A. Vandegrift observed first-hand the way Holcomb handled the Corps' numerous problems. These observations reveal some important features of Holcomb's leadership and organization. Holcomb and his staff at Headquarters faced the nearly overwhelming job of "trying to get two dollars of value out of each one dollar received ...." This took all of Holcomb's ability as a "imaginative planner and administrator" to overcome external budgetary obstacles. He took several steps to minimize the problems of appropriations. First, he demanded that his division chiefs document every "jot and title" of their projected expenses. When testifying before Congress, he never bluffed or overestimated the importance of a given request. On the contrary, Holcomb admitted any lack of justification within his projections when questioned by legislators. He then sought a satisfactory answer for the legislators as soon as possible. Holcomb's fiscal thoroughness and honesty won him respect with Congress. Thus, when the votes occurred, Congress was inclined to be sympathetic to the Corps' plight.[2]

INTERNATIONAL TENSIONS AND CREATION OF THE RAINBOW PLANS

The Japanese protested the 1938 Hepburn Board's recommendations—especially the fortification of Guam and other western Pacific islands. The Japanese recognized the strategic significance of American bases in the Pacific. Japan's own Mahanian strategy called for securing Guam, Wake, and Midway; in this respect, the Japanese Navy formed a "faithful mirror image of its American opponent in strategy." In pursuit of their Greater East Asia Co-Prosperity Sphere, the Japanese also continued their conquest of China with impunity. As early as 1938, the Japanese mobilized to control the valuable natural resources of South East Asia. Meanwhile, tensions in Europe also escalated as Nazi Germany occupied Czechoslovakia. As the world moved toward war, the Americans remained aloof in their isolationism. Although the United States Fleet was moved to the Pacific and Naval talks with the Britain's Royal Navy commenced, even such token moves as concentrating the fleet in the Pacific badly stretched Naval resources.[3]

Thus, serious threats on the European continent and in the western Pacific had made the ORANGE plan obsolete. It had presumed a unilateral American conflict with Japan. The growing probability of war with multiple enemies and allies mandated more flexible contingency plans, resulting in the approval of the five RAINBOW Plans in June 1939. These plans—and their de facto alliances that they implied—drastically transformed American strategy. For example, according to RAINBOW 2, Anglo-French forces focused against Germany; and by default, the task of confronting the Japanese fell to America.[4]

While the new RAINBOW Plans significantly altered American grand strategy, they did not appreciably alter the Marine Corps' mission within this strategy. The Navy intended to deploy defense battalions at Midway, Pearl Harbor, San Diego, and Parris Island. In time of war, these would be "temporary" deployments. If attacked, defense battalions would resist enemy assault until relieved by the fleet. All plans assumed the Pacific fleet would quickly and decisively relieve the island outposts. Or, in an offensive Naval campaign, the defense battalions would accompany amphibious forces and secure newly-seized islands from counterattack. In the ensuing island-hopping campaign, the defense battalions would advance with the amphibious forces. In either event, Navy planners slated Army units to provide "permanent" garrisons as the Corps' forces moved forward. Consequently, under RAINBOW, the Corps' mission still consisted of amphibious assault and base defense.[5]

To fulfill the latter mission, Holcomb ordered the formal organization of four defense battalions. He designated the FMF's 1st and 2nd Battalions, 15th Marines as the "nuclei of the four Defense Battalions." Due to severe manpower limitations, the battalions would receive thirty percent of their personnel from regular units and the remaining seventy percent from the reserve. However, months passed before adequate men and matériel were brought together to form a single defense battalion.[6]

BUREAUCRATIC AND FISCAL PROBLEMS

Fortification of island bases had been recommended by the Hepburn Board but moved slowly, if at all. In mid-1939, Marine and Naval officers toured several Pacific islands. They envisioned Wake and Johnston as "advanced Fleet Air Bases," outposts for the U. S. Fleet, and communication relays. As of early August, their reports titled "The Defense of Wake" and "The Defense of Palmyra" repeated Naval strategists' time-honored base defense theory: the Japanese must be denied the use of these islands. As a corollary, the strategists expected an offensive campaign against the Japanese. Strategically, possession of these bases were a zero-sum game, an equally time-honored vestige of the ORANGE Plans. In reality on August 31, 1939, CNO Harold Stark criticized Naval preparedness in a report to the Secretary of the Navy. One of the "critical deficiencies" found by his report "was the lack of Pacific bases west of Hawaii." In addition to emphasizing the defensive aspects of the Corps' mission, Stark's report also cited the Navy and Marine Corps' complete inability to seize island bases.[7]

Even though a defense battalion's manpower was meager in numbers, the proposed reassignment of several thousand nonexistent Marines to four new units proved impossible. Likewise, defense battalions required a significantly greater number of weapons and amount of ammunition than other Marine units. Defense battalions combined artillery batteries and heavy infantry in a "composite infantry-artillery unit." The weapons and equipment to supply these heavily armed units either did not exist or dated back to World War I. To solve this dilemma in the fall of 1939, the War Department agreed to place Army units under the Navy's command—thus relieving the Marines of security and garrison "duties at all Naval stations outside the continental United States except those Marines in China and the Philippines." These Naval stations included Coco Zolo, Balboa, Pearl Harbor, Guam, Guantanamo, and Sitka. Some 900 Marines were transferred to duty in defense battalions. Furthermore, the War Department agreed to contribute 59,000 rounds of 3" AA (High Explosive) ammunition and some 5 million rounds of .50 Cal AA (Ball, Armor Piercing, and Tracer) to the Corps.[8]

However, exchange of ideas and promises at the departmental level did not filter down to the service level. In one case, when the Army inventoried their ammunition, the Corps' requirement constituted "serious reduction of critical items in the hands of Army troops and ammunition reserves." The request for 59,000 rounds of 3-inch AA (High Explosive) constituted 25 percent of the Army's total stock; and the request for 1 million rounds of .50 Cal. (Armor Piercing) constituted 40 percent of total stock. Hence, the Army refused to comply with the Corps' ammunition request.[9] In another case, some Navy officers refused to support procurement of supplies to fortify and defend Pacific islands like Wake. Despite the emphatic recommendations of the Hepburn Board, Wake did not receive its allotment because CNO Leahy and Rear Admiral Ingersoll, his assistant, had previously believed that this atoll offered little except "as merely an air transit point reinforcing Guam."[10]

The disruption caused by the formation of defense battalions was not limited to relations with the other services. Internally, the Corps also experienced the frustration of robbing-Peter-to-pay-Paul. Four defense battalions required approximately 2900 Marines. Because it had been designated to include defense battalions, the FMF would therefore have to cut its total amphibious assault force of almost 4100 to 1200 Marines. Holcomb attempted to alleviate this drain by transferring 900 Marines from Naval station garrisons to the FMF, calling up 6600 reserves, and enlisting 3600 recruits. On paper, Holcomb's solution more than compensated for personnel shortages. But, in reality, his solution was overly optimistic. First, Holcomb fully expected to reduce enlisted reservists by at least 20 percent due "to various reasons" like age or physical unfitness. Second, the need for more promotions to warrant officer (WO) lowered the regulars' total by 12 percent. Finally, until they gained proper training and experience, the raw recruits greatly diminished the FMF's level of combat readiness. As a result, demand for troops was much greater than supply.[11]

EXPANSION FOSTERED BY OUTBREAK OF WORLD WAR II

During its struggle for resources, an international incident pushed the Corps toward expansion. On September 1, 1939, Nazi Germany's invasion of Poland shattered the delusion of peace. War, possibly engulfing the world, ominously loomed on the horizon. President Roosevelt responded by proclaiming American neutrality. The majority of Americans favored such an aloof reaction to the outbreak of war. Yet German aggression also gradually raised public support for increased defensive preparedness. RAINBOW 2 went into effect. This plan resembled ORANGE but anticipated multiple allies and enemies. So the military benefited from what Acting Secretary of the Navy Charles Edison called "this present emergency."[12]

As the German *blitzkrieg* raced across Europe, President Roosevelt declared a "limited" national emergency. Justifying the need for a strong defense became easier. By October 1939, CNO Stark decided to station a defense battalion in San Diego rather than the previously assigned Midway. The Navy could speedily move a defense battalion to Midway in a crisis as soon as the atoll was properly fortified.[13]

Before September 1939, Holcomb had concentrated on guaranteeing the Corps' mere existence. But, the outbreak of war in Europe served as a turning point for the Corps. Existence or purpose ceased to be issues. Expansion surfaced as the major issue—not if but how much and how fast. Yet the reality of unpreparedness continued because only two defense battalions could be fully equipped instead of the original four. In addition, the Corps lacked Marines to staff the most basic posts at Pearl Harbor. Construction had been scheduled; but no substantial fortifications existed in late 1939 on Midway—let alone more westward islands like Wake or Guam.[14]

MARINE REACTIONS TO WAR

Thomas Holcomb's finely tuned publicity machine capitalized on the opportunity provided by the war-torn international arena. According to Marine Corps historian Robert Lindsey, "the uneasy situation of the mid to late 1930s marked a sort of milestone for Marine Corps public relations." Holcomb shifted his emphasis in publicity to recruitment. He utilized an impressive array of media to broadcast the Corps' essential role and attract recruits. As a rule, Holcomb did not envision "cheap" propaganda as publicity; on the contrary, he sought "legitimate publicity." For example, he provided Marine guards for the 1939 World's Fair even though this duty stretched his already limited personnel.[15]

The 1939 film *The March of Time* was one of the most striking pro-Marine advertisements. It showed precision marching units from the Corps, the Coast Guard, and the National Guard. One observer noticed that the Marines exhibited a "fine appearance and military bearing." Moreover, they "put the Coast Guard and National Guard to shame with their precise drill and manual." Members of the Marine Corps Headquarters Staff also responded positively because they believed *The March of Time* gave the Corps a positive image. To help create such favorable publicity, Holcomb cultivated well-placed contacts within the media like Henry R. Luce of Time and Life, Inc. Holcomb also called on former leathernecks like Sam Meek of J. Walther Advertising Company for assistance. James Roosevelt epitomized the Marine-media connection. He was son of the President, an officer in the Marine Corps Reserve, and a vice president in Samuel Goldwyn's production company. Thus, James Roosevelt was in a position to promote the Corps' image. But, even with the publicity efforts of Holcomb, recruitment remained slower than expected.[16]

Recruitment was not the only area making little headway. Procurement and organization also floundered. Everything from housing to ammunition to weaponry required attention. Holcomb apologized to his unit commanders for all the "difficulties in meeting demands ...." For example, Holcomb intended to station the 1st Defense Battalion at Pearl Harbor as had been previously planned. However, immediate setbacks included a shortage of housing and an a overabundance of duties for the 725 men once they arrived. In theory, a defense battalion's functions did not entail security duty for a given base. These units were designed as rapid deployment defense detachments. But, in practice, the Marines helped provide security for Pearl Harbor.[17]

Organizationally, a defense battalion's armament incorporated both anti-aircraft and coast defense guns. Preparation to repel air, sea, and amphibious assaults overwhelmed the normal chain of command. Typically, a lieutenant colonel commanded a battalion. But, numerous "weapons functions" and "widely separated stations" required not only a more senior officer of colonel's rank but also a possible redesignation of defense battalion to "defense regiment" or "composite artillery regiment." Likewise, a need arose for more lower-ranking officers and more decentralized command structure. This flexibility would allow elements of a given defense battalion to operate semi-autonomously. This command structure worked well in the defense of Wake Island in December 1941. During the Japanese amphibious assault, elements of the 1st Defense Battalion lost contact with the command post. These Marines continued to hold their positions and even counterattacked against the landing force.[18]

MORE EXPANSION

During early 1940, the international situation worsened. German forces successfully crushed Anglo-French forces in Europe and crippled their ability to meet Japan's threat. Realizing this, Japanese forces found little resistance in their conquests in Asia. With the fall of France in May of 1940, American strategists grew desperate. The contingency plans moved to a worst case RAINBOW 4: "A unilateral defense of the Americans extended to include the area below 10 degrees south latitude and the eastern Atlantic." The key terms in this summary of RAINBOW 4 were "unilateral defense" of the western hemisphere. Because of England's impotence, the United States of America stood truly "isolated" between the double menace of Germany in Europe and Japan in the Pacific. Roosevelt reacted by restricting trade with Japan and keeping the U.S. Fleet stationed as a deterrent at Pearl Harbor. To help relieve America's strategic crisis, Army Brigadier General George V. Strong drafted the "Strong Memorandum," calling for a "purely defensive posture in the Pacific." Roosevelt was not alone in his reactions against the increasing international tensions. Pro-security Senator Edward R. Burke and Representative James W. Wadsworth pushed for mobilization via conscription.[19]

Because of multiple threats and corresponding military weakness, Congress passed the "Two Navy Act" in July 1940. Among other items, this act authorized construction of more than 300 new warships and nearly quadrupled the Navy's budget from $1.8 billion to $6.3 billion. This act also included significant increases in Corps strength: expenditures rose from $33 million in 1940 to $67 million in 1941, and manpower rose from 28,000 Marines in 1940 to 64,000 Marines in late 1941. Congress' willingness to raise $1 billion in new taxes testified to the public's greater concern for national security.[20]

With the geometric increase of defense budgets in fiscal year 1940 and later in 1941, an influx of personnel occurred. The military experienced incredible expansion as a result of the Second World War: 200,000 men in 1939 to over 12 million men in 1945. For its part, the Marine Corps grew from 16,000 men in 1936 to over 300,000 in 1943. Smooth expansion did not occur. The services risked promoting officers of questionable competence. According to diplomatic historian Mark Stoler, a so-called "managerial revolution" occurred. It modeled itself on the massive industrialization in the early twentieth century. According to the "managerial revolution," leaders took a decentralized, or line and staff, approach to operations. Holcomb was emblematic of this managerial style.[21]

HOLCOMB'S MANAGEMENT STYLE

Holcomb split Marine Corps Headquarters into several divisions and departments: Plans and Policies, Aviation, Public Information, Reserve, Recruiting, Inspection, Personnel and Supply. Each performed specific tasks.[22] Alexander Vandegrift illustrated Holcomb's technique in the following:

> The general was not one to waste time with unnecessary administrative routine. When a problem arose he assigned it to the concerned division; if it involved several divisions, then Holland [Smith] or I was to have the answer. Reasoning that a given problem normally concerned one division more than another, Holcomb saw little value in today's highly touted staff conferences which he considered a waste of time ... Once satisfied with a solution, he accepted it as his decision and responsibility, then stuck to it, often moving mountains in its accomplishment.[23]

Thus, Holcomb employed a decentralized or, line and staff, style of management. This corresponded with a Commandant's established function as administrator rather than field commander. Theoretically, delegation of authority allowed Holcomb to concentrate on matters external to the Corps. These included interservice and civil-military relations.[24] As Holcomb's assistant, Alexander A. Vandegrift performed the duties of a chief of staff. He handled the micromanagement of the Corps. Vandegrift's quote also typified the admiration for Holcomb felt by many of his subordinates.[25]

In dealing with Congress, the President, or the American public, Holcomb and his subordinates demonstrated the qualities of salesmen. In this capacity, they extolled the virtues of the Corps. Periodically, influential members of Congress and the Roosevelt administration inspected Marine training camps and other facilities. During these visits, they witnessed precision drills, observed target practice, and were wined and dined, courtesy of the Corps. Marine hosts went out of their way to accommodate the Congressmen during the personal tours. On one occasion, Brigadier General William P. Upshur discovered that Representatives Scrugham and Plumley "had had some military service." Upshur "bore down on that angle and talked to them `as one soldier to another' which they very much liked—it tickled them." During this same visit, Secretary of the Navy Charles Edison attended some of the Marine activities. Upshur took advantage of the opportunity to supply Edison with a memorandum listing items needed to raise the FMF to a higher level of preparedness.[26]

Even with the encouraging budget hikes, the Corps remained inadequately prepared for its responsibilities. Expansion proved no small task. The strength of the mid-1940 Corps stood at 28,000 men and officers. Holcomb could expect further expansion and mobilization. He predicted an increase to 34,000 by October. In answer to a request by Representative Carl Vinson, he also projected additional growth to 50,000 men for Fiscal Year 1941. Three reasons insured the Corps' growth. First, by law, the Corps maintained its personnel at twenty percent of the Navy's personnel. Second, the international situation worsened with the collapse of European allies. Third, the newly appointed Secretary of the Navy Frank Knox pressured a reluctant President Roosevelt into authorizing the Corps' expansion by 15,000 men. Evaluating Knox, Holcomb "confidentially" described him as a "real, take charge" administrator. Consequently, Holcomb felt that the Corps found itself in a "most healthy situation ... that has not existed for many years." Defense battalions also benefited from expansion with an augmented force of 6,600 men in six units.[27]

GROWING PAINS

Holcomb however faced serious obstacles in training raw recruits and the recalled reservists and retirees. Because Marine recruits at Parris Island skyrocketed from 190 to 1,600 per month, difficulties in rank allocation and promotion arose. Many newly formed units lacked competent officers and NCOs. For their part, raw recruits went through an abbreviated basic training supervised by generally inexperienced drill instructors (DIs). It was noteworthy that, before the per-World War II expansion, DIs had often served ten to fifteen years in the Corps before assuming their duties in basic training. The shortage of NCOs compounded the overabundance of ill-prepared Marines. No more did the problem of stagnation of promotion exist as it had during most of the interwar years. Quickened training resulted in Marines of questionable quality being trained by DIs of questionable qualifications and being commanded by officers of questionable ability. If that did not place enough pressure on the establishment, the Corps trained with equipment of First World War vintage. Consequently, units were being stationed with questionable combat readiness.[28]

In an effort to quicken yet not cheapen the training process, recruits received thorough marksmanship and physical training while at boot camp in San Diego or Parris Island. This inculcated Marines' most basic skills as riflemen. Upon arriving at their initial assignments, the new Marines learned the advanced tactics and field skills at new bases like Camp Pendleton. In the officers' ranks, various schools drew particular types of officers. Reserve officers enrolled in the Junior and Base Defense Weapons Courses at Quantico; regular officers attended the Senior Course at Quantico; and, the Basic Course at Philadelphia drew from the batch of new second lieutenants. Whether officers or enlisted men, new recruits in the late 1930s enjoyed one advantage. They had all been hardened while enduring the Depression years. As for motivation behind their enlistment, the recruits eagerly joined the Corps as much for employment as for patriotism.[29]

Growing pains were not limited to the enlisted ranks. Newly commissioned reserve and regular officers had little time to learn their staff responsibilities before facing either promotion or transfer to another unit. As a result, three distinct groups of officers emerged in the Corps: career officers, green Officers Candidate Course (OCC) graduates, and reserve officers of questionable qualification. A reserve WO or senior NCO could be called back to active duty as a captain. In this capacity, he was equal in rank to a twenty-year captain with tours of duty in Nicaragua and China and perhaps a stint at the Naval War College; in addition, this new captain commanded lieutenants fresh out of OCC and senior NCOs with fifteen years experience. Because of the rapid manpower build-up, experience and qualification in the chain of command was problematic.[30]

Because he was responsible for internal supervision of the Corps, Vandegrift attempted to reconcile rank with competency. Determining the truly competent—whether younger or older—leaders took time. Officers and senior NCOs had to be tested under stress to prove their mettle. If an error in assignment were to occur, experienced WOs or NCOs would accompany less experienced commissioned officers. By waiting, Vandegrift hoped to avoid the mistakes of 1917 in which experienced officers led inexperienced NCOs. Another delicate situation occurred; career Marines sometimes resented being out-ranked by reservists called to active duty. To alleviate this tension, Holcomb shrewdly removed the "R" from the USMCR designation of the reserves. Consequently, all were Marines without distinction.[31]

In an effort to quickly train a greater number of officers, the Platoon Leaders Classes (PLC) at Quantico and San Diego expanded under the auspices of the Marine Corps Schools (MCS). A forerunner of Officer Candidate School (OCS), the PLC was originally directed in 1935 toward college graduates. Relatively certain of expansion by the late thirties, Holcomb enlarged the PLC and thus enlarged the pool of officers from 1936 through 1940. A more rigorous training program provided the Corps with a batch of "high quality" reserve officers. But, when the "first ripples of mobilization started" in July 1940, the PLC failed to provide enough officers capable of handling combat leadership. Thus, PLC eventually evolved into the Officer Candidate Course (OCC). This demonstrated that expansion was taken seriously by the officers in the Corps: "the OCC had the task of assessing the candidates for leadership potential and discharging those men who did not measure up to the physical demands or emotional stress of combat officership." In addition to a comprehensive study of drills, infantry weapons, and small unit tactics, a Marine's officer training included a "rudimentary knowledge of leadership skills."[32]

In addition to manpower, the Corps faced other critical deficiencies. Fulfilling the dual mission of amphibious assault and base defense presented the Corps with another perplexing dilemma. In this respect, procurement in mid-1940 proved no better than a year or ten years earlier. Successfully establishing itself as the ideal force for both base defense and amphibious assault proved to be a pyrrhic victory in some ways. Supplying either amphibious or defense missions stretched the Corps' already meager resources; acquisition of the necessary manpower to undertake both missions proved logistically impossible.

As of June 1940, less than half of the total items requested by the FMF were on hand. For instance, the FMF had only 900 machine guns (of any size) "on hand" out of approximately 3300 machine guns of their "total requirement;" furthermore, no 37mm anti-tank guns, 60 mm mortars, 37 mm anti-aircraft guns, or 20 mm anti-tank guns existed. These anti-aircraft and anti-armor items were essential to both amphibious and defense operations. Ammunition proved to be the most grievous area of unpreparedness. Of projectiles above .50 caliber, 2.5 units of fire were "on hand" and 4.5 units were "on order" out of the 22.5 units required for full combat readiness. In the areas most relevant to amphibious assault, less than twenty percent of the necessary equipment had been filled or ordered. Finally, future "on order" items due for the most part in 1941 or 1942 failed to match the FMF's total requirement. Consequently, speaking of Marine Corps preparedness in 1940 was not as appropriate as speaking of unpreparedness primarily because appropriations and equipment allocations had not increased proportionately to military threats.[33]

WAR IN EUROPE WORSENS

On the international scene, the Battle of Britain raged throughout July 1940. Even with additional American financial and material aid, the fate of Great Britain hung in the balance. France's capitulation reduced Great Britain to a purely defensive position. The United States of America stood alone. In the Pacific, the situation was even more grim. Vichy France ceded rights to Southeast Asian bases to the Japanese. Britain could send no strong opposing force to confront the Japanese in that arena. Thus, according to Allan R. Millett, "by default the United States, not yet involved in the European war, became the leader in the coalition against Japan."[34] In this quote, "coalition" must be interpreted broadly because no formal coalition existed. Roosevelt could do little more than increase support for China, use economic sanctions to deprive Japan of the raw materials in Southeast Asia, trade antiquated American destroyers for British bases in the western hemisphere, and begin establishing an advanced base on Midway. Congress voted to raise taxes to pay for a two-ocean Navy including 15,000 aircraft.[35]

The Corps benefited slightly from this movement toward preparedness. Because of heightened international tension, a detachment from the 1st Defense Battalion finally landed on Midway in July 1940. Other elements of this "overextended" unit occupied Palmyra and Johnston islands. However, the long-awaited deployment of a defense battalion drained the Corps' scarce resources.[36]

While the seriousness of the international situation may not have been fully known, concern filtered down to the Corps. The need for a large, powerful Corps grew proportionately with this Japanese threat. To fulfill the anticipated strategic mission, the Marine Corps made great effort bringing the FMF to full battle readiness. According to mid-1940 projections, the FMF would make up half of the Corps' total strength or 25,000 enlisted men. This in turn would be subdivided into force headquarters totaling 99 men, six defense battalions totaling 4,344, three Marine brigades totaling 16,557, and two aviation wings totaling 4,000. Within the FMF, the twin mandate of island seizure and base defense formed a "division of labor." Of course, this remained only a projected distribution. By fall 1940, a 50,000 man Corps corresponded to the increasing threat in the Pacific. And, by April 1941, the need had subsequently grown to 75,000 men.[37]

RAMIFICATIONS FOR DEFENSE BATTALIONS

Although the unit had been acclaimed as the culmination of base defense theory, few people seemed to know the exact rationale behind a defense battalion. Defense battalions had roots reaching back to the turn of the century. The name "defense" was more than a mere public relations ploy. The defense battalion also fulfilled viable tactical and strategic functions. Marine First Lieutenant Robert D. Heinl, Jr., picked up the gauntlet to define and to justify the defense battalion in his 1940 article "Marine Coast Artillery: The Defense Battalions." He originally intended to publish his piece in the Coast Artillery Journal. But, due to the "restricted nature of the information contained" in his article, Marine Corps Headquarters blocked its publication and distributed Heinl's article directly to Marine officers.[38]

Reminiscent of Ellis's work twenty years earlier, Heinl's article outlined the basic tenets of base defense: strategic mobility and tactical immobility. While heavily armed and well-trained, defense battalions were not large enough to repel a "hostile main effort." Heinl did not expect them to repel a determined invasion. He assumed that any force large enough to overpower a defense battalion would necessarily "attract correspondingly strong elements of the U.S. Fleet." The defense battalion would be most effective against small flotillas composed of cruisers or lighter vessels and small amphibious forces of battalion size. In retrospect, the defense of Wake Island verified Heinl's basic premise.[39]

Heinl also explained some practical aspects of base defense. For shore-to-ship warfare, a defense battalion employed the old Navy 5-inch gun. With minor modification for coast defense, this weapon's high muzzle velocity and advanced fire control equipment gave it good accuracy and long range. The 5-inch gun also proved to be easily transported, handled, and installed. A defense battalion's three or four batteries either operated jointly or, if communications with headquarters were lost, individually. 3-inch anti-aircraft, searchlight, and sound detector batteries completed the artillery component. Defense battalions utilized two machine gun batteries for beach and anti-aircraft defense. As with the rest of the unit, economy of force was a premium in the machine gun batteries. By following the Corps' principle that every Marine was a riflemen and by borrowing from the Navy's "battle-stations" method, each Marine in a defense battalion had his regular duty and a combat duty during action. Thus, the defense battalion was designed to achieve self-sufficiency as well as eliminate overhead personnel for transportation, communication, or installation.[40]

In his closing paragraph, Heinl proclaimed that the defense battalion "liberates infantry and other artillery units of the [FMF] from any inherent responsibility for the protection of bases." But, efficiency only occurred on paper. The Corps still lacked adequate personnel and equipment. In fact, during the latter half of 1940, no fully equipped, fully manned defense battalions existed on a given base. The equipment did not exist; and training occupied personnel.[41]

THE 1940 ELECTION AND THE SHIFT IN PUBLIC OPINION

Whereas the tension in the international arena made military appropriations a little easier, a strong isolationist strand still ran through the American public. Funds were not made available in a timely fashion to meet growing military threat. The Corps' growth and military readiness hinged on generous appropriations. For the defense battalion, the Corps, and the American military as a whole, the 1940 national election proved to be the major watershed in American diplomacy and strategy.[42] Because elected officials had been hamstrung by an isolationist American public, the election gave breathing room to officials sympathetic to the Corps' plight. No longer did Roosevelt and the Members of Congress need to worry as much about offending isolationist voters. Their isolationist tone slowly shifted to a non-belligerent interventionist tone. On a practical note in December 1940, President Roosevelt reappointed Thomas Holcomb to a second term as Commandant of the Marine Corps. This vote of confidence empowered Holcomb to continue working for a strong Corps.[43]

Holcomb immediately recognized the 1940 election's significance and capitalized on it in two ways. First, he attempted to gain publicity. However, not all the publicity was so positive. For the Navy Day issue of *Life*, the Corps had received scant coverage. Holcomb complained in a letter to the publisher that the issue "disappointed" him because it was "not of a character particularly calculated to increase [the Corps'] prestige." After Holcomb's complaints, the publishers of *Life* agreed to run a separate story on the Corps in early 1941.[44]

Perhaps because the publishers of *Life* felt guilty about their limited coverage of the Corps, a "grateful" Holcomb later received excellent exposure on the November 11, 1940 cover of *Time*. This story was in press before the election occurred. The "National Defense" cover story also painted the Corps in a positive light. Beginning with basic training, raw recruits became inculcated "with the conviction that a Marine is better than any other fighting man ...." Moreover, the transformation from civilian into Marine bordered on a religious experience. Intermingled with anecdotes about bravery and history, the article stated that "the Corps has been built to function with a minimum of trouble ... to be prepared for anything." In addition to the publicity from *Time*, the Corps also gained favorable exposure from a program on NBC radio commemorating the Corps' birthday on November 10.[45]

Second, Holcomb wrote newly elected Senators and Representatives to congratulate them on their victories and plug the Corps as the ideal force. In one letter to Senator-elect Ralph O. Brewster of Maine, Holcomb congratulated Brewster on his victory and expressed great enthusiasm for his appointment to the Senate Naval Affairs Committee. Holcomb wrote a similar letter to Senator-elect C. Wayland Brooks of Illinois, a former Marine. Holcomb hinted that Brooks should also attempt to gain a place on the Senate Naval Affairs Committee.

CONCLUSION

1939 and 1940 proved to be eventful years for the United States Marine Corps. Following the Hepburn Board's recommendation, defense battalions became a reality. However, an isolationist American public and its Congress nullified any effort to raise the defense battalions—or the whole military—to combat readiness. Too few men had too many responsibilities. As with most military achievements during this period, the Corps and the defense battalion gained support primarily because of international pressures: war in Europe and threats in the Far East. Germany's smashing victories led the American public and the Federal Government to the realization that the globe, as well as the number of American allies, shrank with every passing day. Likewise, Japan's continued aggression also prompted an increased interest in military preparedness. The Corps benefited in part because American strategy called for a defensive war in the Pacific—the perfect assignment for a defense battalion. Support for military preparedness peaked with the election of 1940. Following this election, establishing the importance of the Corps and the defense battalion ceased to be an issue. New administrative and bureaucratic challenges faced Holcomb in 1941 as he and the Corps attempted to attain preparedness.

CHAPTER 3

THE RACE FOR PREPAREDNESS, 1941

INTRODUCTION

Following the 1940 election, Congress appropriated and Roosevelt approved funds for military expansion more readily. The American public gradually supported preparedness.[1] This final chapter recounts Commandant Thomas Holcomb's ongoing struggle to gain men and equipment in 1941. The military's speculative tone changed to a confident tone. As a result, the Marine Corps' situation improved immeasurably as the drive for preparedness began. Plan DOG and the ABC Talks detailed the Anglo-American response to the Axis threat. The Corps maintained a high profile in each of these contingencies. Training and deployment of amphibious forces and defense battalions inched forward.

Holcomb primarily dealt with bureaucratic and logistical challenges as he attempted to balance the offensive and defensive components of the Corps' mission. Responsibilities expanded more quickly than resources became available. The Corps remained perpetually six months behind. Holcomb also contended with the Navy's slow supply system and competed with the Army and the Allied powers for scarce resources.

NEW WAR PLANS AFFECT THE CORPS

During the final weeks of 1940, CNO Harold R. Stark completed work on an assessment of America's future strategies. His "Stark Memorandum" outlined four scenarios labeled Plans A through D. He grappled with the problem of economy of force. In the foreseeable future, the American military did not possess the resources to fight two major wars on two fronts. Severely limited military power forced Stark to choose from among several unsatisfactory options.[2]

Plan A called for a unilateral defense of the Western hemisphere. An isolationist American public remained relatively detached from the global conflict as found in RAINBOW 4. Plan B called for an offensive war concentrated in the Pacific against Japan with Dutch and British assistance. This plan assumed that Allied assistance would be modest because the British and Dutch resources focused on Europe. Likewise, Britain would be left to fend for itself. Plan C called for equally strong efforts in both Atlantic and Pacific. This would have been impossible because of the scarcity of American resources. Finally, Plan D called for a concentrated effort against Germany and a defensive stance against Japan in the Pacific. Economy of force could thus be directed against Germany and Italy. Later known as Plan DOG, this last contingency rested on at least two assumptions: first, war appeared probable and perhaps inevitable; and second, the European theater represented the more immediate priority. Obviously, the Marine Corps figured heavily in each contingency.[3]

The military had long expected a conflict between the United States and Japan in the Far East. Prior to the attack on Pearl Harbor, Naval strategists expected a Japanese strike in the Western Pacific. During his tenure as a Vice Admiral before World War II, Ernest J. King observed, "the trend of events following the outbreak of war in Europe indicated that the war would eventually engulf the United States and become global in all its aspects."[4] King made his observation as part of a 1944 report. Although hindsight undoubtedly skewed his perspective, the statement certainly contained shades of fatalism and determinism. Expectations of war were not limited to the highest-ranking officers in the Navy; they trickled down through the Corps' ranks.[5]

In his introduction, CNO Stark recognized that America's "national objectives" necessitated the "preservation of the territorial, economic, and ideological integrity of the United States." Of all adversaries, Germany was the most immediate threat. Achieving "national objectives" compelled America to sustain Britain against almost certain defeat by Germany. Stark predicted that a British defeat would relegate America to Plan A, a purely unilateral defense of the Western Hemisphere. However, following Plan DOG's victory in Europe, forces could be concentrated in a Pacific offensive. In his conclusion, Stark recommended joint talks with British, Canadian, and Dutch military planners.[6]

Plan DOG formed a nucleus for the American-British-Canadian Talks (ABC-1) lasting from January through March of 1941. The resulting report outlined America's support of the Allied Powers. Plan DOG modified American strategy for working with the Allies and revised RAINBOW 5 to account for France's capitulation. Fighting Germany was the highest priority. In the Pacific, the United States would attempt to avoid war with Japan. In the event of hostilities, American Naval forces would maintain a "strategic defense" which included "limited" or "tactical" offensives in the Central Pacific. Allied planners conceded that ABC-1 meant the probable losses of Guam and the Philippines. They also hoped their "strategic defense" would divert Japanese forces from East Asia and relieve the pressure on the British forces remaining there. By May 1941, the Joint Army-Navy Board accepted Plan DOG and ABC-1. In the long term, ABC-1 encapsulated the Allies' war-winning strategy.[7]

While Roosevelt never officially approved Plan DOG or ABC-1, Stark and Naval strategists proceeded with their specific recommendations. Stark redirected the war effort to "Germany First" and de-emphasized the Navy's initial role in the Pacific. However, in the event of America's entrance into the war, the Marine Corps' role in the Pacific remained the same or perhaps expanded. Two "tasks" specifically were given to the Corps: first, defense of outlying island bases like Wake, Midway, Samoa, Palmyra, Johnston, and Guam; and, second, seizure of island chains like Carolines and Marshalls. In a "strategic defense," both "tasks" were intertwined. Amphibious assault and base defense were important because the Corps had to capture and sustain possessions.[8]

High-level correspondence confirmed that both seizure and defense of advanced bases received great attention. In a letter on 10 January 1941, Admiral Robert Ingersoll ordered Holcomb to organize six new defense battalions as soon as he had completed the organization of the 1st and 2nd Marine Divisions. The amphibious assault arm of the FMF held top priority, and base defense held second priority. Six new defense battalions raised the total to twelve with a complement of over 10,000 Marines.[9]

In a different communication, Stark also ordered the 3rd Defense Battalion to Midway and the 1st Defense Battalion to be divided between Palmyra and Johnston. A sense of urgency was evident in still another of Stark's letters:

The existing situation requires the Johnston and Palmyra Islands be provided as expeditiously as practicable with defensive garrisons capable of defending the installations and operating forces present against minor raids.[10]

Island bases constituted the outer line of American defenses.

Admiral Husband Kimmel, Commander in Chief of the Pacific Fleet (CINCPAC), concurred with Stark's directives. Moreover, Kimmel wholeheartedly advocated "permanent" garrisons and "accelerated" construction on these islands. On a more practical level, the bases needed refrigerators, distilling equipment, and other transportation and support material. In general, the construction on the Western Pacific bases was less than thirty percent completed as of March 1, 1941. A report by the Navy's Bureau of Yards and Docks optimistically estimated completion dates in late 1941 and early 1942.[11]

From the evidence, several conclusions can be drawn. First, Plan DOG and ABC-1 clearly enhanced the Corps' position in American strategy. Second, although it had top priority, the amphibious assault mission did not monopolize all resources. Plan DOG's proposed "strategic defense" assumed that island bases would change hands. These bases either needed to be held if in American possession or retained if taken from Japan. Either way, defense battalions would prove essential. Thus, base defense clearly shared importance with amphibious assault; defense complemented seizure. Third, American commanders presumed that a war with Japan would erupt sooner or later. In fact, a February 1941 letter from Kimmel to Stark warned, "that a surprise attack (air, submarine, or combined) on Pearl Harbor is a possibility."[12]

EQUIPMENT AND PERSONNEL INADEQUACIES

Under the auspices of increasing preparedness, Holcomb requested authorization for 71,000 regular and reserve Marines by 1942. This number far exceeded the 45,000 regular and reserve Marines mobilized by early 1941. As always, Holcomb repeatedly complained that existing men and equipment lagged far behind the actual requirement. The Navy also began pressuring the War Department and the Army to fill the Corps' requests for ammunition and weapons. To make matters worse, the Corps depended almost entirely on the other services because it did not have its own ordnance department to develop new weaponry. Holcomb and Stark even solicited aid from Representative Carl Vinson, Chairman of the House Naval Affairs Committee and long-time patron of the Corps.[13]

The Corps drifted slowly toward combat readiness in accordance with the Plan DOG and the RAINBOW Plans. By March 1941, seven defense battalions had been formed, and Midway had received its full complement of Marines. This was encouraging. Yet much work still had to be done to achieve full combat readiness. Only five of the seven defense battalions "could be considered as being reasonably well trained and prepared to carry out the mission of defending small bases against minor raids." The two units lacking "certain major items" depended on the Army to relinquish it equipment. According to one estimate, bringing the defense battalions to full readiness would take four months.[14]

The FMF's 1st and 2nd Marine Divisions also faced severe shortages. These two amphibious assault units possessed only fifty percent of their manpower and forty percent of their required equipment. A report on the FMF's deficiencies predicted a sixteen month delay until 1 July 1942 before one hundred percent manpower could be achieved.[15] The amphibious assault units' lengthier "speed of attainment" seemed to indicate the importance of base defense because defense battalions had a shorter "speed of attainment." Naval strategists have long assumed that the Western Pacific bases would be attacked first and therefore would need to be supplied more quickly.

With war looming on the horizon, Roosevelt initiated the Lend-Lease Program in March 1941. The program was a blessing and a curse. From the British perspective, Lend-Lease placed America's potential industrial might squarely behind their war effort. However, from the American military's perspective, helping the British created another level of competition and exacerbated already critical shortages of both men and equipment. The industrial expansion siphoned off available resources: "a handicap which [the Corps] never encountered before." Whereas America's armed services formerly competed among themselves for limited men and equipment, Lend-Lease amplified their rivalry. For instance, acquiring comfortable shoes, let alone modern weapons or sufficient ammunition, posed problems for the Corps.[16]

MEETING THE CHALLENGES

While Holcomb unsuccessfully endeavored to overcome the Corps' external challenges, he entrusted Alexander Vandegrift with finding solutions to the Corps' internal challenges. Delegating responsibility and authority to his subordinate demonstrated Holcomb's consistent line and staff management. The Corps' internal difficulties included command structure and training, among others.[17]

Vandegrift planned to reform the FMF's command structure. He wanted to place Marine divisions directly under a fleet's commander. By localizing control, Vandegrift hoped to avoid the inherent communication and administration problems caused by exercising leadership from several thousand miles away. He also introduced some important reforms within the Marine divisions of the FMF. When they had been trained, competent officers would form "a tactical command" made up of the commanding officer (CO) and a small tactical staff. Of course, having a "staff in being" required officers to hold the positions. By spring of 1941, not enough officers had been trained or commissioned.[18]

Both the Marine Corps and the Navy still lacked competent officers and enlisted men to fill vacancies. Possible solutions to the Corps' manpower shortages floated around Vandegrift's office. Because recruitment sagged during the spring months, Marine Brigadier General Charles Price recommended that former leathernecks be offered re-enlistment and placed on active duty at posts near their homes. From his perspective as CO of the Department of the Pacific based in San Francisco, manpower limitations severely handicapped operations. His enlisted men shouldered double duty in security guard companies and in the FMF. Price theorized that the re-enlisted Marines could perform these extraneous guard duties. Consequently, his Marines could focus on training in amphibious assault and base defense, their primary duties.[19]

Vandegrift also continually faced a scarcity of experienced officers. Anecdotes abound concerning their quick transfer from assignment to assignment. To help fill the officers' ranks, college seniors were eventually commissioned in the Marine Reserve. Having inexperienced officers was considered as bad as having no officers. Without sufficient training, they hurt the morale of their subordinates and incurred the jealousy of their peers. To avoid placing inexperienced officers on line, Vandegrift directed recent college graduates to complete the Platoon Leaders Course before receiving their commissions. Afterward, they went on active duty and attended courses specifically designed for Reserve officers.[20]

PUBLICITY AND RECRUITMENT

Holcomb concentrated his persona; energies on external challenges like public relations, interservice relations, and Congressional relations. With war looming larger in 1941, Holcomb intensified his public relations campaign. He spent much of his time generating a positive image for the Corps. Holcomb expanded his message from an almost purely defensive accent to include the offensive capabilities of the Corps.[21]

From his position as the Corps' chief salesman, Holcomb employed "every means available to keep the Marine Corps favorably before the people." He took full advantage of the networks which had been developed over decades. Holcomb contacted J. G. Harbord, a fellow leatherneck at RCA, to help improve the Corps' image and therefore increase recruitment. Harboard, in turn, tried to arrange radio programming which presented the Corps in a positive fashion. Elsewhere, Holcomb used his contacts to obtain "colorful Marine Corps scripts" by the "finest writer in radio" and "excellent pictures" in periodicals like *Life* and *Saturday Evening Post*. These carefully refined sights and sounds helped perpetuate the Corps' image as America's premier fighting force. Military historian Craig M. Cameron claims that Marine recruits "were looking to join the service of Captain Flagg and the old `Horse Marines' of Peiping."[22]

Holcomb articulated his publicity agenda in a letter to Admiral Ernest J. King, CINCLANT. With regard to an article forthcoming in *Life*, Holcomb wrote, "it is fine clean publicity ... of a type that could not be bought and will serve, I believe, a very useful purpose." The article explicitly highlighted the Corps' ability "to carry on amphibious operations as part of the Fleet." The pictures and written word held a deeper, implicit message: the Corps was being portrayed as an integral part of the Navy and the Fleet.[23]

Because publicity had become so complicated, Holcomb replaced the Publicity Section in the Adjutant and Inspector's Division with the autonomous Division of Public Relations (DPR) in July 1941. Its responsibilities included supervising and coordinating all of the Corps' publicity efforts.[24] According to General Vandegrift,

> All officers are urged to submit direct to the Director of Public Relations any idea they may have as to fostering public relations or furthering publicity, and also to submit in the same manner photographs, etc., which are believed to have news value.[25]

Thus, the DPR also formed the focal point for generating ideas for better publicity. Under its auspices, the Corps' recruitment was stimulated by publishing the magazine *The Marine Recruiter*. It is noteworthy that, by delegating the task of Corps public relations, Holcomb applied line and staff management. Instead of giving more responsibilities to his "old-line administrative departments," Holcomb made "new-line staff agencies" like the

DPR directly responsible to his Commandant's office. This methodology helped smooth the roughness inherent in rapid expansion.[26]

Because the Lend-Lease program lured potential recruits to industrial jobs with high pay and draft exemptions, recruiting methods themselves also changed. Competition for available manpower became very intense as 1941 wore on. Interservice resentment increased as the Navy, Army, National Guard, and Coast Guard scoured areas for recruits. Recruiting officers expanded their search from the usual urban centers to include the rural areas. No stone was left unturned.[27]

During the Depression, recruiting had run on a shoestring budget. Service in the Corps appealed to young men by offering employment, excitement, and travel. But, by mid-1941, this message was not alluring enough. The cost per recruit gradually formed the basis for determining the cost of recruiting. Before increasing the number of recruits, the required amount of money and resources needed to be increased.[28]

In response to the new difficulties in recruitment, Charles Price offered a comprehensive program to enhance the process. He wanted recruitment to become intertwined with public relations. Specifically, Price argued that Marine recruiters should target small towns with advertisement in local newspapers and broadcasting on local radio networks. This more "individual" touch included publicizing news about a leatherneck that would interest people in his hometown. Price also advocated revisions in Corps' posters. He believed that the poster should tell a story and illustrate life in the Corps. Attention was given to the smallest detail. To appease mothers of young men under eighteen years old, Price advised that Corps publicity should soft pedal the fierce looking Marine prepared to stick a bayonet in someone. The boys may like that idea but, if you have to get the mother's consent, she will not consent to having her little boy jab human beings with a bayonet.[29]

Recruitment did not end when recruits completed basic training. The new Marines themselves served as potential recruiting tools. They should be stationed far away from their homes and encouraged to write home about the new lives. In this way, a "little brother and schoolmates may become inoculated with the Marine bug." Finally, Price believed that retired leathernecks could be effectively utilized as recruiters. He submitted his recommendations in a long letter to Alexander Vandegrift.[30] Presumably, Vandegrift would have then forwarded Price's suggestion to Holcomb and the DPR. Line and staff management would therefore have functioned up and down the chain of command.

Young men who joined the Corps before Pearl Harbor confirm the effect of publicity on recruitment. In a recent survey of the 7th Defense Battalion, Marines cited a number of "reasons" for enlistment. Of thirty-five single responses, patriotism and duty motivated twenty to join the Corps. Among the remaining fifteen responses, six indicated a desire "to be Marines:" either the appeal of an "elite" organization or the desire to avoid being drafted in the Army. It can be inferred from the majority of responses that the Corps presented a certain image that influenced young men. Finally, only five responses indicated a need for employment. The relatively few recruits merely seeking employment in the Corps verified that less "gung ho" young men had other options for mere employment. Conversely, young men who joined the Corps before Pearl Harbor wanted to be Marines.[31]

During the first six months in 1941, defense battalions floundered. Manpower and equipment hovered around half strength. Construction of advanced bases fared even worse. As of April, construction on Guam had not been started. Construction on Midway and Wake had begun but did not become remotely suitable for defense until the fall of 1941. The Corps and its resources were spread too thinly. Operational demands accelerated more quickly than the Corps' ability to keep pace.[32]

At the highest level of Naval leadership, grandiose schemes evolved like the "Plan for the Expansion of the U.S. Marine Corps, Report and Recommendations by the General Board, May 6, 1941." This report recommended that the Corps should grow to 123,000 officers and men. This total included from twenty to forty percent "replacement personnel for casualties in the initial stages of combat" and an extra ten percent active personnel "not available" for active duty. Consequently, the fully combat ready strength of the Corps would be closer to 75,000 Marines. This figure was the strength for Fiscal Year 1942 previously authorized on 18 April 1941. Its combat ready strength should also have been reduced by thirty to fifty percent.[33]

According to the "Plan for Expansion," the FMF would be expected to climb over 61,000 officers and men. Of these, 29,000 would serve in the 1st and 2nd Marine Divisions. Defense battalions were given 6,800 Marines for eight units, a comparatively small amount. They were subdivided into four light and four heavy units. Light differed from heavy defense battalions in their armament. The former employed 5-inch guns and lighter AA guns; the latter would upgrade to the 6-inch gun and heavier AA weaponry. Deployment depended on the situation and the particular base.[34]

Significantly, the "Plan for Expansion" also created support units for the defense battalions. 12,500 Marines would serve in separate infantry battalions, balloon barrage squadrons, and base defense aircraft groups. Of these complementary units, the separate infantry battalion served as a strategic reserve in an "active defense." This enabled a defending force to make strong counterattacks if an enemy's assault force established a beachhead. Most Marines in regular defense battalions had their primary battle assignments in artillery or machine gun batteries. As a result, the defense battalion had few men for a strategic reserve. On big islands like Samoa, planners believed that infantry support would be essential for a successful defense. Together with the defense battalions, the support units totaled nearly 20,000 Marines or one third of the whole FMF. Even in May 1941, advanced base defense remained a vital part of the Corps' mission.[35]

In its recommendations, the "Plan for Expansion" called for the Corps' growth "as rapidly as it is practicable to procure, equip and train the necessary officers and men." The plan also recommended that "replacement supplies" be stockpiled for an emergency. However, the "Plan for Expansion" had no foundation in reality. Not enough money was appropriated. Some of the units like the separate infantry and the balloon barrage battalions were never deployed. Throughout the summer of 1941, the Corps hovered around 50,000 Marines.[36]

Severe shortages persisted in weaponry, ammunition, and equipment for defense battalions. As of May 1941, only two defense battalions, the 2nd and the 4th, could be considered equipped and trained. But their readiness would drain other units of experienced Marines and essential material. The remaining units like the 3rd and the 5th lacked both "considerable equipment" and sufficient training. In the 5th's case, "considerable equipment" included everything from 3-inch AA guns to height finders to sound locators. Ammunition was the most conspicuous shortage. The 2nd and 4th Defense Battalions could have achieved combat readiness within one month's time if only the necessary ammunition was *made available*." Combat readiness would have also meant depriving other units of their experienced officers and NCOs.[37]

To be combat ready, a defense battalion required 22.5 units of fire. According to one pre-war estimate for 3-inch AA guns, 22.5 units of fire translated into 75,000 rounds shared among twelve guns. This amount would last approximately four months in time of war. In actuality, a single defense battalions' "on hand" ammunition averaged 1.5 units of fire. Or, in terms of time, a single defense battalion could fight about ten days before running out of ammunition.

No relief could have been obtained from other military services. As of May 1941, the Navy's inventory of 3-inch AA ammunition "on hand" was approximately 13 units of fire. The Army's inventory "on hand" included 42 units of fire. Army and Navy stockpiles combined for 55 units of fire. Thus, bringing a single defense battalion up to full combat readiness depleted forty percent of the military's 3-inch A.A. ammunition. Marine defense battalions hardly had adequate ammunition with which to practice, let alone fight a battle. Little hope was in sight with May's "production of about 20,000 rounds per month ... reaching 100,000 a month by end of year."[38]

Members of the 7th Defense Battalion verify the Corps' poor state of readiness. This unit's veterans paint an abysmal picture of the western Pacific island of Samoa. Veterans described their level of readiness as "very low," "ragged," and "lousy." Worse still, the unit was spread too thinly to be able to adequately protect Samoa, a large island. Deficiencies in weapons and ammunition contributed to the 7th's pathetic state. Artillery included reconditioned 6-inch guns and World War I-vintage Lewis guns. These "archaic" and "obsolete" weapons were "the Army and Navy's cast offs." Neither radar nor weapon cleaning equipment existed.[39]

Both quality and quantity of ammunition contributed to the 7th's lack of readiness. Marines did not trust their ammunition because of its "unpredictable quality." For some weapons, the 7th only possessed 1000 rounds or enough for 72 hours of combat. Edward T. Peniston, an enlisted man in the 7th, recalled that his unit was not capable of any sustained defense against a determined assault in 1941.[40]

Although many problems existed, at least two areas within the Corps were encouraging. First, "morale was excellent." When questioned about the effect of low manpower and old equipment on the 7th's morale, Harold M. Benscoter said "Hell, we were Marines." Other veterans concurred that they took "pride in surviving insurmountable odds." Sharing the shortages of material and the hardships of boot camp actually raised their level of morale and *esprit de corps*.[41]

Early in 1941, Congress appropriated $15 million to purchase land at New River in North Carolina. This new 24,000-acre base provided the necessary space to house and train the thousands of recruits expected in the coming months. The FMF used New River for its offensive and defensive exercises. Marines practiced assaulting the beaches with Naval gunfire and close air support. They tested landing craft. On the defensive side, base defense tactics also improved. Marine gunners operated all types of AA and anti-ship artillery. New River was ideal because use of live ammunition did not endanger civilians or property. Thus, this instillation simultaneously accommodated amphibious assault and base defense. New River's training facilities enabled the Corps' to train up to 2,500 new recruits per month. Still, fiscal setbacks continued to plague the Corps as Congress slowly appropriated the money to construct the facilities.[42]

BARBAROSSA'S RAMIFICATIONS FOR THE CORPS

On 22 June 1941, Adolf Hitler surprised the world by launching BARBAROSSA, the attack on the Soviet Union. Nazi Germany sortied an enormous force: more than 150 divisions with more than three million Axis soldiers along a one thousand mile front. During the summer and fall of 1941, the German army raced across Western Russia and recreated its *blitzkrieg* of 1939. The initial German victories devastated the Soviet Army.

The Russo-German conflict had positive and negative effects on America and Britain. On one hand, it eased the pressure in Western Europe. Because Germany focused so many of its resources against the Soviet Union, England gained valuable breathing room. Conversely, BARBAROSSA allowed also Japan freer movement on the Asian continent. Large segments of the Soviet Army were moved from their positions in Siberia to meet the German threat. These forces had previously deterred further Japanese expansion on the Asia continent. Japan faced a choice: either continue its uninhibited advance in China or turn south toward South East Asia. If Japan had chosen to continue its northern advance in China and Siberia, then the Western Allied forces would have gained some time. Instead, Japan chose a southward advance, which brought an immediate confrontation with America and England.[43]

President Roosevelt reacted to Japan's aggression in China by freezing Japanese assets in America. He hoped this action would discourage further movement into South East Asia, but Roosevelt's action initiated a *de facto* embargo on American oil exports to Japan. Far from discouraging any further advances, Japanese expansion surged forward at a greater pace. A thirst for natural resources increased as its reserves dwindled.[44]

RAINBOW 5 took effect because of the serious shift in the Far East. On 21 July 1941, CNO Stark distributed copies of the "U.S. Pacific Fleet Operating Plan - Rainbow Five (Navy 0-1, Rainbow Five)." This plan's "Estimate of Enemy Action" speculated that Japan would initially capture Malaysia and the Philippines, thus disrupting Allied communication and supply lines. Meanwhile, a Japanese offensive against China would be sustained but at a lower level of intensity. Finally, the Japanese Navy would destroy Allied forces.

Among other specific details, RAINBOW 5 assumed that the Japanese military would attempt to insulate itself behind a network of fortified island bases including Guam, Wake, Midway, Samoa, and others. This assumption further justified Corps' dual mission. By placing defense battalions on these Western Pacific islands in harm's way, RAINBOW 5 validated America's need for advanced base defense. To bolster the number of defense battalions, Naval planners even laid plans for the U.S. Army to train and deploy its own version of defense battalions.[45]

Like ABC-1 and Plan DOG, RAINBOW 5 called for a concentrated offensive against the German and Italian forces in Europe. In the Pacific, American forces would employ a strategic defense with limited tactical offensive operations. The Pacific strategy entailed containing Japanese expansion and maintaining supply lines to the Far East and Australia.[46] Whether in the ORANGE, RAINBOWS 1 through 4, DOG, or ABC-1 plans, the Marine Corps' dual mission changed very little even though America's war plans changed significantly. The FMF continued to be the amphibious assault and base defense arms of the Pacific Fleet. Both parts of the dual mission served important strategic purposes: defense complemented offense.[47]

"ARE WE READY—III"

The answer to the September 1941 report "Are We Ready—III" was negative. In early June, Commandant Holcomb had reported the Corps' most "critical deficiencies" to CNO Stark. These included every conceivable weapon from M1 Garands to 155 mm howitzers, tanks to aircraft. As for ammunition, Holcomb did not quote specific numbers or types; he bluntly wrote that "shortage exists for all the above weapons." In addition, the Corps lacked a full quota of "all major items of fire control equipment and accessories …." The essential instruments included altimeters, height finders, observation telescopes, aiming circles, automatic gun control equipment, data transformation systems, flank spotters, and directors for both 3-inch and 37 mm AA guns.[48]

By the end of summer in 1941, some progress toward readiness apparently had been made. Personnel shortages saw significant improvements. The Corps rose to an active strength of 56,000 officers and men. Congress appropriated and President Roosevelt approved funds to bring this figure to 75,000 by 31 March 1942. With subsequent authorization by the Congress and the President, the "Are We Ready - III" report expected the Corps' strength to reach 104,000 by 31 March 1942 including 62,000 Marines assigned to the FMF. Six new defense battalions and a 3rd Marine Division were planned.[49]

During the summer and fall of 1941, the Corps experienced net gains of 2,500 recruits per month and 1000 newly commissioned officers per year. These numbers supported manpower projections for 75,000 Marines by the end of March 1942. While the Corps experienced increases in absolute terms, its expanding duties greatly exceeded its 1941 strength of 56,000 Marines in relative terms.[50]

Limited manpower was not the Corps' only inadequacy. Supplies of equipment and weapons saw little improvement. The FMF boasted no more than 10 units of fire for any particular weapon. Most units like the 1st, 3rd, 4th, and 6th Defense Battalions averaged only 3 or 4 units of fire. Shortages in .50-caliber ammunition were especially grievous. In holding an island, 50-caliber machine guns performed two vital functions as anti-aircraft and beach defense weapons. The "Are We Ready - III" report of September 1941 confidently predicted that the "situation in regard to Weapons and Ammunition of the defense battalions in the Pacific area will approach a reasonably satisfactory condition by 1 January 1942." The confidence proved to be in vain.[51]

Full combat readiness remained further from being a reality than a few months and a few units of fire. Any suspicion that requirements were exaggerated should be viewed in light of the Corps' starvation-level of supplies. Chronic shortages had troubled the Corps for more than two decades. When requesting funds for men and equipment, Holcomb always tried to honestly present his budget. As seen before, his reputation for requesting only necessities often gained Congressional favor.[52]

EVIDENCE OF THE DEFENSE BATTALION'S SIGNIFICANCE

Because defense battalions absorbed men and equipment, it is believed that these units negatively affected the Corps' overall readiness. According to eminent Marine Corps historian Allan R. Millett, the defense battalion was the product of "military faddists." These units as well as aviation units depleted the Corps of its "most intelligent recruits." As a result, the FMF's amphibious assault units "would have to do with few skilled officers and noncommissioned officers." To Millett, this drain on manpower by special units like the defense and raider battalions became more "onerous" after the United States entered the war.[53]

However, Millett's "onerous" label does not apply to defense battalions prior to the attack on Pearl Harbor. While amphibious assault had a higher priority, advanced base defense also played an absolutely essential role in America's Pacific strategy. RAINBOW 5 anticipated a standoff in the Pacific and highlighted the importance of base defense. Therefore, the fact that so many Marines were assigned to defense battalions ultimately testified to these units' significance.

A few Marines also assert that serving in defense battalions hurt individual careers. Their assertions are over-generalizations. Before Pearl Harbor, most Marines did not connect slow promotions with their service in the defense battalions. The demand for officers and senior NCOs was so great during the pre-war expansion that almost anyone could quickly rise in rank. Admittedly, defense battalions saw little action when compared to amphibious assault forces after America entered the war. A command at Midway in 1944 might have been a dead end. However, this did not imply that a Marine's career would be hurt by a tour of duty with a defense battalion, especially in 1941. Individuals held a number of assignments throughout their careers, any of which could help or hurt a career. If service in defense battalions truly did hurt careers, more evidence would exist in the sources.[54]

Herein lies compelling evidence for the significance of defense battalions. These units drew a large number of qualified Marines because of the advanced base defense's vital strategic mission. In December 1941, 5,265 Marines served in the six defense battalions. This figure amounted to twenty percent of the 26,560 Marines in the entire FMF. Serving in a base defense unit required specialized mathematical skills for radar operation, AA direction, and coastal artillery direction. Not every Marine possessed these skills. Thus, defense battalions might be considered "elite" units.[55] If the defense battalion had been a mere fad, then it would not have drawn such qualified Marines.

Manpower distribution offers more evidence for base defense's importance. A defense battalion required a CO of colonel's rank. Commandant Holcomb justified this requirement in the following: "The fire power of a defense battalion is greater than that of an Army AA regiment, and, in personnel and weapons, compares favorably with a light cruiser." In addition, a tour with the defense battalion offered a potentially independent command, a opportunity which every Marines desired. Such high ranking officers as Colonels were in great demand elsewhere.[56] Once again, if the defense battalion had been a fad, then it would have neither warranted nor attracted colonels as COs. Therefore, the quality and rank of the Marines within the units further testified to the defense battalions' significance.

LACK OF READINESS IN NOVEMBER AND DECEMBER, 1941

During the latter half of 1941, publicity remained positive and effective. Holcomb continued to promote the Corps wherever and whenever possible. Although recruitment declined slightly in October, the Officer's Candidate School churned out many qualified, albeit inexperienced, Marine officers. Likewise, the Corps stayed on a time table to reach its 75,000 plateau by the end of March 1941. This was only a small comfort because the international situation grew increasingly threatening.[57]

As November 1941 passed, incessant equipment shortages and sluggish equipment distribution plagued the Corps and its defense battalions. A CINCPAC report titled "Study on Defenses and Installations at Outlying Pacific Bases" updated the developments on Wake, Midway, Palmyra, and Johnston islands. All these advance bases urgently needed more .50-caliber machine guns for anti-aircraft defense and .30-caliber machine guns for beach defense. In Wake Island's case, eighteen .50-caliber guns comprised its "present actual armament." This amounted to only thiry percent of Wake's allotment of sixty .50-caliber guns, CINCPAC's recommended number "required for a reasonable defense under our assumptions."[58]

On numerous occasions, Admiral Kimmel pleaded with CNO Stark for support: "I do not think that the few machine guns required by these battalions should be spared from other activities and I hope that the ammunition situation will be remedied very shortly." In a similar letter, Kimmel lamented that "it is practically certain that these units will fight before the Army will and their needs must be given priority." Despite such high level patronage, Wake's Defense Battalion was not given priority quickly enough. Independent sources in the Corps confirm these and other deficiencies on Wake.[59]

The "Study on Defenses" detailed much more than current state of readiness. It also underscored the significance of advanced bases to America's Pacific strategy, a postulate dating back to the Spanish-American War. The study acknowledged that an attack on Wake was a foregone conclusion. Naval strategists expected that the Japanese Navy would attempt to capture and convert Wake into their own advanced base. The 1st Defense Battalion's primary objective was holding the island. If its holding action proved impracticable, then the secondary objective became the slowing of a Japanese advance. Simultaneously, the U.S. Pacific Fleet would be sortied to fight the Japanese and relieve Wake. Clearly, possessing Wake Island was a zero-sum game.[60]

The situation in the Far East steadily deteriorated as the Japanese moved to open conflict with the United States. The distant rumblings of war grew more immediate to the Corps' lower ranks. Captain James Devereux, CO of the 1st Defense Battalion on Wake, received an "Ultra Top Secret" communication which bluntly warned that the "international situation indicates you should be on alert." Despite this foreboding message, Devereux received no reliable intelligence on an attack. The attack on Pearl Harbor provided the biggest warning.[61]

During the final days preceding the Japanese attack on Pearl Harbor, Admiral Kimmel attempted in vain to get more troops, weapons, and equipment to Midway and Wake. A few obsolete Brewster Buffalos were delivered to the bases. Kimmel even requested that the Army dispatch troops to support the Marines already on the island bases. His assistance proved to be too little and too late. By the time Wake's reinforcements were scheduled to arrive, the war had started.[62]

Woodrow Kessler, a Marine stationed with the 1st Defense on Wake, speculated that his unit's pathetic state of readiness resulted not from any lack of imagination, intelligence, or foresight on the part of the military but rather from the uncertainties of the appropriations from a pacifist-oriented society and Congress.[63]

Kessler blamed the American public and civilian leadership for the military's lack of preparedness. Most Americans probably could not conceive that Japan was actually capable or daring enough to sail several thousand miles across the Pacific to attack Pearl Harbor. While the isolationist feelings and indecisive policies shared some blame, fault also rested with the military and its logistic system. The Army and Navy failed to coordinate a timely transfer of equipment to the defense battalions on the Western Pacific islands. Furthermore, unity of command within the Navy should have averted some problems of logistics and communication. However, the problems occurred just the same.[64]

CONCLUSION

The failure to adequately supply the defense battalions and the rest of the Corps did not result from a lack of effort by Commandant Thomas Holcomb. The Corps controlled too few resources and encountered too many challenges. Disputes among services or individuals undoubtedly contributed to a low level of readiness. Maybe the sluggish wheels of bureaucracy turned too slowly. Both these factors played roles. Most obviously, in examining the Corps' "on order" requisitions and "on hand" inventories, sufficient equipment simply did not exist in late 1941. None of the armed services boasted anything close to full combat readiness. In a memorandum for President Roosevelt dated 27 November 1941, COS Marshall and CNO Stark wrote that "the most essential thing now from the United States' viewpoint is to gain time." As became horribly evident two weeks later, time was not a luxury that America enjoyed.[65]

CONCLUSION AND EPILOGUE

In examining Commandant Thomas Holcomb and the development of defense battalions, this thesis accomplishes two objectives. First, it traces the development of advanced base defense from its inception at the turn of the century to its advent with the defense battalion in 1939. Much more than a fad,[1] base defense constituted the Corps's main mission before World War I. During the 1920s and 1930s, amphibious assault shared the top priority with base defense. Finally, as war erupted in 1939, amphibious assault gradually supplanted base defense as the Corps's premier mission. Yet, this shift in priorities did not marginalize the defense battalion. Defending outlying bases continued to play a vital role in Navy strategy and Marine publicity until the attack on Pearl Harbor.

When war came, 400 leathernecks on Wake proved that a defense battalion was also tactically viable. The 1st Defense Battalion's "tough fighters" held Wake in a spirited, if futile, battle. The Marines repelled an amphibious assault and sank two Japanese destroyers before surrendering with no hope of relief. The stubborn defense of Wake has since become part of Marine lore. It inspired the defense battalion's motto, "Send us more Japs."[2] Later in the war, the units' names were changed to Anti-Aircraft Artillery (AAA) Battalion. The updated versions of the base defense force secured beachheads from counterattack and protected the amphibious assault forces from enemy aircraft.

Second, this thesis establishes Commandant Thomas Holcomb as the Marine most responsible for the Corps's expansion before World War II. Despite all the obstacles facing the Corps, Holcomb did everything within his power to raise the readiness of defense battalions and the Corps. He excelled as a publicist, strategist, and manager. Defense battalions influenced Holcomb's actions in all three areas. Defensive vocabulary appeased America's isolationist tendencies; Naval strategy in the Pacific demanded defense battalions complicated the Corps's attempts to obtain and distribute resources.

Holcomb guided the Marine Corps's massive expansion from just over 17,000 Marines in 1936 to nearly 65,000 in late November 1941 and nearly 300,000 when he retired at the end of 1943. Beyond his involvement with defense battalions, he also supervised the development of amphibious assault forces. From Washington, Holcomb coordinated America's counter-offensive across the Pacific. Perhaps military historian John W. Gordon pays the most eloquent tribute to Thomas Holcomb in the following:

> In terms of personality, style, and even intellectual equipment, Holcomb seems to have been not unlike George C. Marshall .... Holcomb was a sort of 'mini-Marshall,' juggling far tinier resources but coping with the vaster geographic sweep of the war in the Pacific. He was, for the Marine Corps, very much its 'true "organizer of victory."'[3]

However, neither the defense battalion's importance nor Holcomb's diligence could bring the Corps to full combat readiness by December 1941. The military was unable to match strategic objectives like defending island outposts with tactical necessities like equipping the defenders. Japan's initial advantage lasted only a short time until the America recovered. During World War II, the Marine Corps's amphibious assault capabilities eventually supplanted base defense in the final defeat of Japan.

APPENDIX 1

COMMANDANTS OF THE MARINE CORPS 1891-1947

Charles Heywood	1891-1903
George F. Elliot	1903-1910
William P. Biddle	1911-1914
George Barnett	1914-1920
John A. Lejeune	1920-1929
Wendell C. Neville	1929-1934
Ben H. Fuller	1934-1936
Thomas Holcomb	1936-1943
Alexander A. Vandegrift	1944-1947

Source: Millett, *Semper*, 653.

APPENDIX 2

STRENGTH OF THE MARINE CORPS 1895-1945

YEAR	OFFICERS	MEN
1895	76	2,100
1898	116	4,700
1900	187	5,520
1910	334	9,267
1916	341	10,056
1918	2,462	72,639
1920	962	16,085
1926	1,177	17,976
1936	1,199	16,040
1940	1,556	26,369
1943	21,938	287,621
1945	37,664	447,389

Source: Millett, *Semper*, 654.

APPENDIX 3

EXPENDITURES BY THE MARINE CORPS, 1933-1943

YEAR	AMOUNT (in thousands of then-year dollars)	AMOUNT (in thousands of 1990 dollars)	PERCENTAGE OF TOTAL NAVAL EXPENDITURE
1933	19,007	191,989	4.4
1934	15,358	150,568	3.8
1935	19,079	181,704	3.3
1936	21,170	199,717	4.0
1937	22,276	202,509	4.1
1938	23,253	215,306	4.0
1939	24,572	231,811	3.7
1940	33,189	310,177	3.7
1941	67,743	599,495	3.0
1942	242,364	1,938,112	2.8
1943	493,144	3,680,179	2.4

Sources: Navy Department, *Naval Expenditures*, 1933-1943, "Statement 1," Summary of Naval Activities; *Historical Abstracts of the United States*; and *Statistical Abstracts of the United States* (1991).

APPENDIX 4

RAINBOW PLANS

RAINBOW 1   A unilateral defense of the Americas above the latitude 10 degrees south

RAINBOW 2   A war in the western Pacific in association with Britain and France, the United States exerting its maximum effort in this theater and not in Europe

RAINBOW 3   A unilateral war in the western Pacific

RAINBOW 4   A unilateral defense of the Americans extended to include the area below 10 degrees south latitude and the eastern Atlantic

RAINBOW 5   A war in Europe in association with Britain and France, whereby United States forces would be sent to the eastern Atlantic and to Europe and/or Africa "in order to effect the decisive defeat of Germany, or Italy, or both."

Source: Major, ibid., 246.

APPENDIX 5

MARINE DISTRIBUTION EFFECTIVE 30 NOVEMBER 1941

Continental U.S. (non-FMF)

Major Marine Corps Bases *	14,707	
Posts and Stations (43)	10,089	
Headquarters and Staff	780	
Recruiting (4 Districts)	847	
Total	26,423	41 %

Overseas (non-FMF)

Posts and Stations (24)	3,367	
Tactical Units **	5,498	
Shipboard Detachments	3,793	
Total	12,658	18 %

FMF, Continental U.S.

1st MarDiv	8,918	
2d MarDiv (less dets)	7,540	
2d DefBn	865	
1st MAW	1,301	
2d MAW	682	
Misc.	633	
Total	19,939	31 %

FMF, Overseas

5 Defbns (Pacific)	4,399	
2d MAW (elements) (Pacific)	733	
2d MarDiv (elements) (Pacific)	489	
Total	5,621	9 %

GRAND TOTAL	64,641	

* Quantico, Parris Island, San Diego, Camp Elliot, New River

** 4th MAR (Philippines), 801; 1 SepBn (Philippines), 725; 1st MarBrig(Prov) (Iceland), 3,972.

Source: Hough, ibid., 56.

BIBLIOGRAPHY

ABBREVIATIONS

MCG: *Marine Corps Gazette*

MA: *Military Affairs*

USNIP: *United States Naval Institute Proceedings*

JMH: *Journal of Military History*

PRIMARY SOURCES

ARCHIVAL MATERIAL

National Archives. Record Group 80. General Records of the Department of the Navy. 1900-47. GB 425.

National Archives. Record Group 80. General Records of the Department of the Navy. 1900-47. GB 432.

National Archives. Record Group 80. General Records of the Department of the Navy. General Correspondence of Chief of Naval Operations and the Secretary of the Navy. 1900-47.

National Archives. Record Group 80. General Records of the Department of the Navy. General Correspondence of Chief of Naval Operations and the Secretary of the Navy. 1940-47.

National Archives. Record Group 127. Records of the United States Marine Corps. Division of Plans and Policies. War Plans Section. 1926-42.

National Archives. Record Group 127. Records of the United States Marine Corps. Division of Plans and Policies. General Correspondence. 1921-43.

National Archives. Record Group 127. Records of the United States Marine Corps. General Correspondence. Adjutant and Inspector's Office. 1913-32.

National Archives. Record Group 127. Records of the United States Marine Corps. Division of Plans and Policies. War Plans Section. 1915-46.

National Archives. Record Group 127. Records of the United States Marine Corps. Division of Plans and Policies. War Plans Section. 1937-40.

National Archives. Record Group 127. Records of the United States Marine Corps. Division of Plans and Policies. War Plans Section. 1940-41.

National Archives. Record Group 127. Records of the United States Marine Corps. General Correspondence. Personnel. 1933-38.

National Archives. Record Group 80. General Records of the Department of the Navy. 1900-14. GB 422.

Naval Historical Center. World War II Command File. Operational Archives.

National Records Center. Accession Number 1277-77-30. United States Marine Corps. History.

PERSONAL PAPERS AND REFERENCE COLLECTIONS. MARINE CORPS HISTORICAL CENTER.

Thomas Holcomb

Melvin J. Maas

Julian C. Smith

Alexander A. Vandegrift

ORAL HISTORIES. MARINE CORPS HISTORICAL CENTER.

Thomas E. Bourke

Wilbert S. Brown

William Buchanan

Lester A. Dessez

James P. S. Devereux

Clifton B. Gates

Charles G. F. Good, Jr.

Samuel B. Griffith, II

Russell N. Jordahl

Francis B. Loomis, Jr.

Henry R. Paige

Omar T. Pfeiffer

Oliver P. Smith

Samuel G. Taxis

William J. Van Ryzin

Robert H. Williams

PUBLISHED DOCUMENTS, MEMOIRS, PUBLISHED LETTERS AND CONTEMPORARY COMMENTARIES

Bland Larry I., and Sharon R. Ritenour, ed. *"The Soldierly Spirit", December 1880-June 1939*. vol. 1. *The Papers of George Catlett Marshall*. Baltimore: Johns Hopkins UP, 1981.

Broadbent, E. W. "The Fleet and the Marines." *USNIP* 57 (March 1931): 369-72

Devereux, John P. S. *The Story of Wake Island.* Philadelphia: Lippincott, 1947.

Eliot, George Fielding. *Defending America.* New York: Foreign Policy Association, 1939.

Fuller, Ben H. "The Mission of the Marine Corps." *MCG* 15 (November 1930): 7-8.

Hinds, A. W. "The Island of Guam as a Naval Base." *USNIP* 41 (May 1915): 449-55.

King, Ernest J. *U.S. Navy at War 1941-1945: Official Reports to the Secretary of the Navy.* Washington: Navy Department, 1946.

Krulak, Victor H. *First to Fight: An Inside View of the U.S. Marine Corps.* Annapolis: Naval Institute, 1984.

Lane, Rufus H. "The Mission and Doctrine of the Marine Corps." *MCG* 8 (March 1923): 6-9.

Lejeune, John A. "The United States Marine Corps, Present and Future." *USNIP* 54 (October 1928): 859-61.

_____. "The United States Marine Corps." *MCG* 9 (May 1924): 250-3.

Neeser, Robert William. *Our Navy in the Next War.* New York: Scribner, 1915.

Neville, W. C. "The Marine Corps." *USNIP* 55 (October 1929): 863-6.

Martin, C. "The Selection and Defense of Naval Bases." *Journal of the United States Artillery.* 35 (January- February 1911): 1-6.

Metcalf, Clyde H. *A History of the United States Marine Corps.* New York: G.P. Putnam, 1939.

Secretary of the Navy. *Annual Reports of the Secretary of the Navy for the Fiscal Year 1937-1942.*

Scammell, J. M. "Our Naval Bases in the Pacific." *Infantry Journal* 30 (January 1927): 19-29.

Vandegrift, Alexander A., and Robert B. Asprey. *Once a Marine.* New York: Norton, 1964.

Williams, Dion. "The Defense of Our New Naval Stations." *USNIP* 28 (June 1902): 182-3.

_____. "The Temporary Defense of a Fleet Base" *MCG* (February 1931): 9-12, 53-62.

OTHER SOURCES

Survey Questionnaire. 79 Marines of the 7th Defense Battalion. Distributed and compiled by David J. Ulbrich.

John Anelick	James Argall
Harold M. Benscoter	Richard G. Blay
George B. Bell	William F. Boston
George M. Bradt	Robert J. Brandenberger
Donald J. Brisbois	Thomas B. Broughton
Salvatore J. Butta	Harry Calcutt
James M. Callender	W. C. Coleman
Thomas L. Crowl	Robert F. Cyperski
William D. Daniels	E. J. Dieckmann
Maurice J. Doucette	R. B. Dunkelberger
William A. Dunn	Will Elder
Frank J. Engelhardt	Charles J. Engelhardt
Warren Ferguson	Morris Farmer
Joseph H. Gagner	Jack T. Gillespie
Maurice J. Gremillon	Sheldon L. Hall
Paul F. Henderson, Jr.	Robert L. High
Alexander B. Hooker	J. F. Ingraham
James La Hart	Dick Lawton
Walter J. Kerr	William H. Killian
Steve Kiraly	Jean P. Kirsch
Hubert M. Larkins	William J. Lewellyn
L. E. Matthews	William McGuire
E. Lesley Medford, Jr.	William M. Meyers
Daniel Montgomery	Denton G. Moulton
Jack N. Murray	J. T. Odom, Jr.
Phil Pacini	Kenneth Patrick
Edward T. Peniston	Charles H. Petersen
Bernard Rabin	William H. Raquet
Odell C. Reid	Truxton Ringe
Franklin S. Ruhl	Eugene Rybinski

Antonio Santaniell

A. G. Smith, Jr.

Joan Sparks (Mrs. Ernest Sparks)

Stanley F. Stockwell

Nicholas J. Sutton

Anthony Teresi

Raymond I. Valente

Edward H. Walker

John H. Wilson, Jr.

Kenneth E. Wire

Abraham Shapp

Arthur F. Smith

Walter Stanley

Otis R. Strong

Verne L. Sutton

John S. Tyrpak

John Volentine

Henry P. Wheeler

Harry R. Wilmoth

George Killen

SECONDARY SOURCES

GOVERNMENT PUBLICATIONS — Articles

Ballendorf, Dirk Anthony. "Earl Hancock Ellis: A Final Assessment." *MCG* 74
(November 1990): 79-87.

Fagan, George V. "FDR and Naval Limitations." *USNIP* 81 (April 1955): 411-8. Heinl, R.
D. "The Cat with More than Nine Lives." *USNIP* 80 (June 1954), 656-71.
Matloff, Maurice. "Prewar Military Plans and Preparations: 1939-1940."
USNIP 79 (July 1953): 741-8.

Morton, Louis. "Origins of Pacific Strategy." *MCG* 41 (August 1957): 36-43.

O'Connor, Raymond G. "Naval Strategy in the Twentieth Century." *Naval War College
Review* 21 (February 1961): 4-12.

Paret, Peter. "The New Military History." *Parameters* 21 (Autumn 1991): 10-8.

"Portraits of the Commandants" *MCG* 59 (November 1975): 31- 97.

Russell, John H. "The Birth of the FMF." *USNIP* 72 (January 1946): 49-51.

Russell, W. H., "Genesis of the FMF Doctrine." *MCG* 39 (November 1955): 16-7.

Stoler, Mark A. "U. S. Civil-Military Relations in World War II." *Parameters* 21 (1991):
60-73.

GOVERNMENT PUBLICATIONS — Books

Clifford, Kenneth J. *Progress and Purpose: A Developmental History of the United States Marine Corps 1900-1970*. Washington: United States Marine Corps, 1973.

Condit, Kenneth W., et.al. *A Brief History of Headquarters Marine Corps Staff Organization*. rev. ed. Washington: USMC, 1970.

Furer, Julius Augustus. *Administration of the Navy Department in World War II*. Washington: GPO, 1959.

Hough, Frank O., et.al. *Pearl Harbor to Guadalcanal*, vol. 1, *History of the U. S. Marines in World War I*. Washington: USMC, 1958.

Kessler, Woodrow. *To Wake and Beyond: Reminiscences*. Washington: USMC, 1988.

Marine Corps Administrative History. Washington: Marine Corps Historical Division, 1946. Typed manuscript.

Matloff, Maurice and Edwin M. Snell. *United States Army in World War II: Strategy Planning for Coalition Warfare, 1941-2*. Washington: OCMH, 1953.

Melson, Charles D. *Condition Red: Marine Defense in World War II*. Washington: MCHC, 1996.

Reserve Officers of Public Affairs Unit 4-1. *The Marine Corps Reserve: A History*. Washington, DC: MCHQ, 1966.

Smith, Gibson B. *Thomas Holcomb, 1879-1965, Register of His Personal Papers*. Washington: History and Museums Division, HQMC, 1988.

Smith, Holland M. *The Development of Amphibious Tactics in the U.S. Navy*. Reprint. Washington: USMC, 1982.

Tyson, Carolyn A. *A Chronology of the United States Marine Corps, 1936-1946, Volume 2*. Reprint. Washington: USMC, 1977.

Updegraph, Charles L., Jr. *U.S. Marine Corps Special Units of World War II*. Washington: USMC, 1977.

PUBLISHED ARTICLES

Chambers, John Whiteclay, II, "The New Military History: Myth and Reality," *JMH* 55 (July 1991): 395-406.

Christman, Calvin L. "Franklin D. Roosevelt and the Craft of Strategic Assessment." In *Calculations: Net Assessment and the Coming of World War II.* ed. Williamson Murray and Allan R. Millett. New York: Free Press, 1992.

Conn, Stetson. "Changing Concepts of National Defense in the United States, 1937-1947." *MA* 28 (Spring 1964): 1-7.

Cosmas, Graham A., and Jack Shulimson. "Continuity and Consensus: The Evolution of the Marine Advance Base Force, 1900-1922." In *Proceedings of the Citadel Conference on War and Diplomacy.* ed. David H. White and John W. Gordon. Charleston, SC: Citidel, 1977.

_____. "The Culebra Maneuver and the Formation of the U.S. Marine Corps' Advance Base Force, 1913-1914." In *Changing Interpretations and New Sources in Naval History.* ed. Robert William Love Jr. New York: Garland, 1980.

Crowl, Phillip A. "Alfred Thayer Mahan: The Naval Historian." In *Makers of Modern Strategy from Machiavelli to the Nuclear Age.* ed. Peter Paret. Princeton: Princeton UP, 1986.

Emerson, Wlliam. "Franklin Roosevelt as Commander-in-Chief in World War II." *MA* 22 (Winter 1958-9): 181-207.

Greene, Fred. "The Military View of American National Policy: 1904-1940." *American Historical Review* 66 (January 1961): 354-77.

Gordon, John W. "General Thomas Holcomb and `The Golden Age of Amphibious Warfare.'" *Delaware History* 21 (September 1985): 256-70.

_____. "The U.S. Marine Corps and an Experiment in Military Elitism: A Reassesment of the Special Warfare Impetus, 1937-1943." In *Changing Interpretations and New Sources in Naval History.* ed. Robert William Love, Jr. New York: Garland, 1980.

Herzog, James H. "Influence of the United States Navy in the Embargo of Oil to Japan." *Pacific Historical Review* 35 (August 1966): 317-28.

Huntington, Samuel P. "Interservice Competition and Political Roles of the Armed Services." In *Total War and Cold War.* ed. Harry L. Coles. Columbus: OSUP, 1962.

James, D. Clayton. "American and Japanese Strategies in the Pacific War." *Makers of Modern Strategy from Machiavelli to the Nuclear Age.* ed. Peter Paret. Princeton: Princeton UP, 1986.

Kohn, Richard. "The Social History of the American Soldier: A Review and Prospectus for Research." *American Historical Review* 86 (June 1981): 553-567.

Love, Robert William, Jr. "Fighting a Global War, 1941- 1945." In In *Peace and War: Interpretations of American Naval History, 1775-1984*. ed. Kenneth J. Hagan. Westport, CT: Greenwood Press, 1984.

Lowenthal, Mark W. "The Stark Memorandum and the American National Security Process, 1940." In *Changing Interpretations and New Sources in Naval History*. ed. Robert W. Love, Jr. New York: Garland, 1980.

Major, John. "The Navy Plans for War, 1937-1941." In *Peace and War: Interpretations of American Naval History, 1775-1984*. ed. Kenneth J. Hagan. Westport, CN: Greenwood Press, 1984.

May, Ernest R. "The Development of Political-Military Consultation in the United States." *Political Science Quarterly* 70 (June 1955): 161-80.

Millett, Allan R. "The American Political System and Civilian Control of the Military: A Historical Perspective." *Mershon Center Position Papers in the Policy Sciences* 4 (April 1979): 1-71.

Morton, Louis. "Interservice Co-operation and Political- Military Collaboration." In *Total War and Cold War*. ed. Harry L. Coles. Columbus: OSUP, 1962.

Rosen, Philip T. "The Treaty Navy, 1919-1937." In In *Peace and War: Interpretations of American Naval History*, 1775-1984. ed. Kenneth J. Hagan. Westport, CN: Greenwood Press, 1984.

Shy, John. "The Cultural Approach to the History of War." *JMH* 57 (October 1993): 13-26.

Simpson, B. Mitchell, III. "Harold Raynsford Stark, 1 August 1939 to 26 March 1942." In *Chiefs of Naval Operations*. ed. Robert W. Love, Jr. Annapolis: Naval Institute, 1980.

Spector, Ronald. "The Military Effectiveness of the US Armed Forces, 1919-39." In *Military Effectiveness Volume II: The Interwar Period*. ed. Allan R. Millett and Williamson Murray. Boston: Allen, 1988.

Stoler, Mark A. "The `Pacific-First' Alternative in American World War II Strategy." *International History Review* 11 (July 1980): 432-52.

Walter, John C. "Congressman Carl Vinson and Franklin D. Roosevelt: Naval Preparedness and the Coming of World War II, 1939-1940." *Georgia Historical Quarterly* 64 (Fall 1980): 294-305.

Weigley, Russell F. "The Interwar Army, 1919-1941." In *Military Effectiveness Volume II: The Interwar Period*. ed. Allan R. Millet and Williamson Murray. Boston: Allen, 1988.

PUBLISHED BOOKS

Baer, George W. *One Hundred Years of Sea Power: The U.S. Navy, 1890-1900.* Stanford: Stanford UP, 1994.

Barlett, Merrill. *Lejeune: A Marine's Life, 1867-1942.* Columbia: University of South Carolina Press, 1991.

Braisted, William Reynolds. *The United States Navy in the Pacific, 1909-1922.* Austin: University of Texas Press, 1971.

Brune, Lester H. *The Origins of American National Security Policy: Sea Power, Air Power, and Foreign Policy.* Manhattan, KS: MA/HA, 1981.

Cameron, Craig M. *American Samurai: Myth, Imagination, and the Conduct of Battle in the First Marine Division, 1941-1951.* Cambridge: Cambridge UP, 1994.

Cressman, Robert J. *"A Magnificent Fight:" The Battle for Wake Island.* Annapolis: Naval Institute, 1995.

Donovan, James A., Jr. *The United States Marine Corps.* New York: Praeger, 1967. Doubler, Michael D. *Closing with the Enemy: How GIs Fought the War in Europe, 1944-1945.* Lawrence: University Press of Kansas, 1994.

Geelhoed, E. Bruce. *Charles E. Wilson and the Controversy at the Pentagon, 1953 to 1957.* Detroit: Wayne State University, 1979.

Hagan, Kenneth J. *This People's Navy: The Making of American Seapower.* New York: Free Press, 1991.

Heinl, Robert Debs, Jr. *Soldiers of the Sea: The United States Marine Corps, 1775-1962.* Baltimore: Nautical and Aviation, 1991.

Huntington, Samuel P. *The Soldier and the State: The Theory and Politics of Civil-Military Relations.* Cambridge: Belknap, 1957.

Isely, Jeter A. and Philip A. Crowl. *The United States and Amphibious War: Its Theory, and Its Practice in the Pacific.* Princeton: Princeton UP, 1951.

Keegan, John. *The Face of Battle.* New York: Penguin, 1978.

Lindsey, Robert. *This High Name: Public Relations and the U.S. Marine Corps.* Madison: University of Wisconsin Press, 1956.

Love, Robert W., Jr. *History of the U. S. Navy.* 2 Vols. Harrisburg, PA: Stackpole, 1992.

Metcalf, Clyde H. *A History of the United States Marine Corps*. New York: G.P. Putnam, 1939.

Miller, Edward S. *War Plan Orange: The U. S. Strategy to Defeat Japan, 1897-1945*. Annapolis: Naval Institute, 1991.

Millett, Allan R. *Semper Fidelis: The History of the United States Marine Corps*. Rev. ed. New York: Macmillan, 1991.

_____. *In Many a Strife: General Gerald C. Thomas and the U.S. Marine Corps, 1917-1956*. Annapolis, MD: Naval Institute, 1993.

Morison, Samuel Elliot. *The Rising Sun in the Pacific: 1931-April 1942*. Boston: Houghton-Mifflin, 1948.

Moskin, J. Robert. *The U. S. Marine Corps Story*. Rev. ed. New York: McGraw-Hill, 1987.

Preston, Richard A., et.al. *Men at Arms: A History of Warfare and its Interrelationships with Western Society*. 5th ed. Fort Worth: Holt, 1991.

Sherrod, Robert. *History of Marine Corps Avation in World War II*. Washington, Combined Force Press, 1952.

Shulimson, Jack. *The Marine Corps' Search for a Mission, 1880-1898*. Lawrence: University of Kansas Press, 1993.

Simmons, Edwin H. *The United States Marines: Their First Two Hundred Years, 1775-1975*. New York: Viking, 1976.

Smith, Kevin E. *Conflict over Convoys: Anglo-American Logistics Diplomacy in World War Two*. Cambridge: Cambridge UP, 1996.

Spector, Ronald H. *Eagle Against the Sun*. New York: Free Press, 1985.

Weigley, Russell F. *The American Way of War: A History of United States Military Strategy and Policy*. New York: Macmillan, 1973; Bloomington: IUP, 1977.

Zimmerman, Phyllis A. *The Neck of the Bottle: George W. Goethals and the Reorganization of the U.S. Army Supply System, 1917-1918*. College Station: Texas A & M UP, 1992.

UNPUBLISHED MANUSCRIPTS

Costello, Daniel Joseph. "Planning for War: A History of the General Board of the Navy, 1900-1914." Ph.D. diss., Fletcher School of Law and Diplomacy, 1968.

Dwan, John Edward, II. "Franklin Roosevelt and the Revolution in the Strategy of National Security: Foreign Policy and Military Planning Before Pearl Harbor." Ph.D. diss., Yale University, 1954.

Enders, Calvin William. "The Vinson Navy." Ph.D. diss., Michigan State University, 1970.

Greenwald, Bryon W. "The Development of Antiaircraft Artillery Organization, Doctrine, and Technology in the United States Army, 1919-1941." M.A. thesis, Ohio State University, 1991.

Infusio, Frank J. "The U. S. Marines and War Planning, 1900-1941." M.A. thesis, San Diego State University, 1974.

Kajiwara, Naoki. "The U. S. Marine Corps and the Defense of Advanced Bases: Evolution of Tactics and Organizations, 1900-1941." unpublished manuscript, 20 August 1994.

Landrum, Susan. "Carl Vinson: A Study in Military Preparedness." M.A. thesis, Emory University, 1966.

Prefer, Nathan N. "An Uncertain Mission: The Role of the U.S. Marine Corps in National Defense, 1880-1947." Ph.D. diss., City University of New York, 1985.

NOTES

INTRODUCTION NOTES

1. Richard A. Preston, et.al., *Men at Arms: A History of Warfare and its Interrelationships with Western Society*, 5th ed. (Fort Worth: Holt, 1991), 5.

2. See Richard Kohn, "The Social History of the American Soldier: A Review and Prospectus for Research," *American Historical Review* 86 (June 1981): 553-567; John Whiteclay Chambers, II, "The New Military History: Myth and Reality," *Journal of Military History* 55 (July 1991): 395-406; Peter Paret, "The New Military History" *Parameters* 21 (Autumn 1991): 10-8; John Shy, "The Cultural Approach to the History of War," *The Journal of Military History* 57 (October 1993): 13-26.

3. For the now-classic example of "new" military history, see John Keegan, *The Face of Battle* (New York: Penguin, 1978). For other more recent works, see Craig M. Cameron, *American Samurai: Myth, Imagination, and the Conduct of Battle in the First Marine Division, 1941-1951* (Cambridge: Cambridge UP, 1994); and, Michael D. Doubler, *Closing with the Enemy: How GIs Fought the War in Europe, 1944-1945* (Lawrence: University Press of Kansas, 1994).

4. Fred Greene, "The Military View of American National Policy: 1904-1940" *American Historical Review* 66 (January 1961): 354-77; E. Bruce Geelhoed, *Charles E. Wilson and the Controversy at the Pentagon, 1953 to 1957* (Detroit: Wayne State University, 1979); Mark A. Stoler, "The `Pacific-First' Alternative in American World War II Strategy" *International History Review* 11 (July 1980): 432-52.

5. Phyllis A. Zimmerman, *The Neck of the Bottle: George W. Goethals and the Reorganization of the U.S. Army Supply System, 1917-1918* (College Station: Texas A & M UP, 1992); Kevin Smith, *Conflict over Convoys: Anglo-American Logistics Diplomacy in World War Two* (Cambridge: Cambridge UP, 1996).

6. Allan R. Millet and Williamson Murray, ed., *Military Effectiveness*, 3 volumes, (Boston: Allen, 1988). For the most part, my thesis is in this genre of studying the peace between wars.

7. Charles D. Melson, *Condition Red: Marine Defense Battalions in World War II* (Washington: Marine Corps Historical Center, 1996). I am also indebted to Mr. Melson for allowing me to see an early draft of his monograph. It is noteworthy that the vast majority of Melson's work deals with defense battalions during World War II. The several pages dealing with pre-World War II development bolster my thesis' argument.

8. John W. Gordon, "General Thomas Holcomb and 'The Golden Age of Amphibious Warfare'" *Delaware History* 21 (September 1985): 256-70. Gordon has a chapter on Holcomb forthcoming in an anthology on Marine Corps Commandants to be edited

by Allan R. Millett and published by Naval Institute Press. I was not able to gain access to this forthcoming work.

9. In his article titled "The New Military History," Peter Paret raises another criticism of this genre: "Official history is written to provide a record, to fix the past firmly in our consciousness, but often also to lay bare the lessons for today and tomorrow that the past is thought to offer." Criticism and second-guessing with benefit of hindsight is not necessarily the task of historians. According to Paret, "this utilitarian spirit, the belief in relevance, seems to be more pronounced in official histories" (Paret, ibid., 12).

10. Allan R. Millett, *Semper Fidelis: The History of the Marine Corps*, rev. ed. (New York: Free Press, 1991), 346.

11. For other works that also emphasize amphibious warfare, see Holland M. Smith, *The Development of Amphibious Tactics in the U.S. Navy*, reprint (Washington: USMC, 1982); John H. Russell, "The Birth of the FMF" *USNIP* 72 (January 1946): 49-51; Jeter A. Isely and Philip A. Crowl, *The U.S. Marine Corps and Amphibious Warfare: Its Theory and Practice in the Pacific* (Princeton: Princeton UP, 1951); Frank O. Hough, et.al., *Pearl Harbor to Guadalcanal*, vol. 1, *History of the U. S. Marines in World War I* (Washington: USMC, 1958); Kenneth J. Clifford, *Progress and Purpose: A Developmental History of the U.S. Marine Corps* (Washington, DC: USMC, 1973); Edwin H. Simmons, *The United States Marines: Their First Two Hundred Years, 1775-1975* (New York: Viking, 1976); and J. Robert Moskin, *The U.S. Marine Corps Story*, rev. ed. (New York: McGraw-Hill, 1987). For a purely narrative history of defense battalions, see Charles L. Updegraph, Jr., *U.S. Marine Corps Special Units of World War II* (Washington: USMC, 1977), 61-73. This chapter does not do justice to the overall significance of the defense battalion. Because Updegraph lumps this unit in with balloon battalions, parachute battalions, and raider battalions, his work perhaps contributes to the notion that defense battalions were fads.

12. In addition to Melson's monograph, see Nathan N. Prefer, "An Uncertain Mission: The Role of the U.S. Marine Corps in National Defense, 1880-1947" (Ph.D. diss., City University of New York, 1985), 68; and Cameron, ibid., 35-7. I use Prefer and Cameron's data and arguments to justify my claim that defense battalions were much more than mere fads.

13. Much of the material from National Archives remained classified until my research visits during spring 1995. Some of the most valuable information was found in correspondence, reports, and inventories. The survey's questionnaires provided both factual and anecdotal elements primarily from enlisted Marines' perspectives. These responses added a human element to my thesis.

14. For example, Frank J. Infusino, Jr., "The United States Marine Corps and War Planning (1900-1941)," (M.A. thesis, California State University, San Diego, 1973). In part, Infusino narrates the development base defense and seizure. His thesis agrees

with much of my thesis' argument but lacks the recently declassified material found in my research. Naoki Kajiwara, "The U.S. Marine Corps and the Defense of Advanced Bases: The Evolution of Tactics and Organizations, 1900-1941," (Unpublished manuscript, 20 August 1994). Kajiwara places base defense in a strategic context and traces the evolution of unit-level tactics and organization of base defense. But, he does not deal with base defense's institutional significance in the Corps' relationship with the Navy, Congress, and the American public. Both Infusino and Kajiwara were invaluable. Graham A. Cosmas and Jack Shulimson, "Continuity and Consensus: The Evolution of the Marine Advance Base Force, 1900-1922," in *Proceedings of the Citadel Conference on War and Diplomacy*, ed. David H. White and John W. Gordon (Charleston, SC: Citadel, 1977). Cosmas and Shulimson examine the history of the advanced base force. While this article is helpful until the Washington Naval Treaty, my research contends that base defense remained very important after 1922.

CHAPTER 1 NOTES

1. The advanced base force had been called a number of names over the decades of its development. These included advance base brigade, advanced base defense regiments, base defense forces, defense detachments, and finally defense battalions.

2. W. H. Russell, "Genesis of the FMF Doctrine," *MCG* 39 (November 1955): 16-7; Millett, *Semper*, 272; Hough, ibid., 7.

3. George Dewey, General Board Report No. 51, 6 October 1900, Archives Branch, Marine Corps Research Center, Marine Corps University.

4. Dion Williams, "The Defense of Our New Naval Stations" *USNIP* 28 (June 1902): 182-3; Frank H. Schofield and E. H. Ellis, "Report of Naval War College Committee on Defense of Guam," 14 April 1913, General Board Subject File (GBSF) 1900-1947, GB 422, Box 120, Record Group (RG) 80, National Archives (NA). Secondary literature also acknowledges Guam's importance in strategy; for example see Louis Morton, "Origins of Pacific Strategy," *MCG* 41 (August 1957): 36-43; Daniel Joseph Costello, "Planning for War: A History of the General Board of the Navy, 1900-1914" (Ph.D. diss., Fletcher School of Law and Diplomacy, 1968), 167-72, 221-4; William Reynolds Braisted, *The United States Navy in the Pacific, 1909-1922* (Austin: University of Texas Press, 1971): 33, 441-52.

5. For Mahan's Naval strategy, see his major works: *The Influence of Sea Power upon History* (Boston, Little: 1890) and *Sea Power in its Relation to the War of 1812*, 2 vols. (reprint, New York: Greenwood Press, 1969). For an overview of Mahan, see Phillip A. Crowl, "Alfred Thayer Mahan: The Naval Historian," *Makers of Modern Strategy from Machiavelli to the Nuclear Age*, ed. Peter Paret (Princeton: Princeton UP, 1986), 444-80. For an excellent commentary applying Mahanian principles to the first half of the twentieth century, see Russell F. Weigley, *The American Way of War:*

A History of United States Military Strategy and Policy (New York: MacMillan, 1973; Bloomington: Indiana UP, 1977).

6. Williams, ibid., 182-3.

7. Williams, ibid., 187-90; C. Martin, "The Selection and Defense of Naval Bases" *Journal of the United States Artillery* 35 (January-February 1911): 2, 6.

8. Naoki Kajiwara, "The U. S. Marine Corps and the Defense of Advanced Bases: The Evolution of Tactics and Organizations, 1900-1941," (Unpublished manuscript, 20 August 1994), 2-3; and Cosmas, "Continuity," 31-3.

9. President, General Board (PGB), to Secretary of the Navy (SecNav), "Duties of Marines and their connection with Advanced Base Outfits," July 21, 1913, GBSF 1900-1947, GB 432, Box 163, RG 80, NA. See also Millett, *Semper*, 271-81; Infusino, ibid., 34-7; R. D. Heinl, "The Cat with More than Nine Lives" *USNIP* 80 (June 1954), 656-71.

10. George Barnett, memo for SecNav, 8 December 1914, GBSF 1900-1947, GB 432, Box 163, RG 80, NA.; Graham A. Cosmas and Jack Shulimson, "The Culebra Maneuver and the Formation of the U.S. Marine Corps' Advance Base Force, 1913-1914," in *Changing Interpretations and New Sources in Naval History*, ed. Robert William Love Jr. (New York: Garland, 1980), 293, 299-306; Melson, ibid., 2.

11. Schofield, ibid., 1-3, 9-15. This report was laced with racist remarks about the Japanese (pp. 1-2).

12. PGB to SecNav, 26 February 1913 op. cited in Costello, 223; A. W. Hinds, "The Island of Guam as a Naval Base" *USNIP* 41 (May 1915): 449-55; Robert William Neeser, *Our Navy in the Next War* (New York: Scribner, 1915), 163-5.

13. Eli K. Cole, lecture delivered at the Marine Corps Barracks in Philadelphia, PA, 19 June 1915, pp. 1-6, File 1975-10, Adjutant and Inspector's Office General Correspondence (A&I) 1913-1932, Box 234, RG 127, NA.

14. George Barnett, memo for SecNav, December 8, 1914, GBSF 1900-1947, GB 432, Box 163, RG 80, NA; John A Lejeune, lecture, "Defense of Advanced Bases by Mobile Forces," 21 May 1915, File 1975-10, A&I, 1913-1932, Box 234, RG 127, NA; Millett, *Semper*, 284.

15. Gibson B. Smith, *Thomas Holcomb, 1879-1965, Register of His Personal Papers* (Washington: History and Museums Division, HQMC, 1988), 1-2; Cameron, ibid., 22-5; Ronald Spector, *Eagle Against the Sun: The American War with Japan* (New York: Free Press, 1985), 24; Prefer, 110-4. For a general overview, see Millett, *Semper*, 288-318.

16. Earl H. Ellis, *Advanced Base Operations in Micronesia* (1921; Washington: GPO, 1992), vi; Millett, *Semper*, 218-9; Russell, "Genesis," 18.

17. Joint Board (JB) to Secretary of War (SecWar), "Strategy of the Pacific," 18 December 1919, op. cited in Infusino, ibid., 140-2; Chief of Naval Operations (CNO) to MGC, "Function of the Marine Corps in War Plans," 28 January 1920, and memo from CNO to MGC, January 28, 1920 op. cited in Infusino, ibid., 152-3; GB to SecNav, 10 August 1932, "Examination of the Organization and Establishment of the United States Marine Corps," GBSF 1900-47, GB 432, Box 163, NA; Hough, ibid., 8.

18. John A. Lejeune, "The United States Marine Corps, Present and Future" *USNIP* 54 (October 1928): 861; memoir of Russell N. Jordahl (1970), MCOHC, 13; Clyde H. Metcalf, *A History of the United States Marine Corps* (New York: G.P. Putnam, 1939), 542-3; Millett, *Semper*, 322-8. For a recent biography, see Merrill Barlett, *Lejeune: A Marine's Life, 1867-1942* (Columbia: University of South Carolina Press, 1991).

19. Memoir of Samuel B. Griffiths, II (1968), MCOHC, 29; Ellis, *Advanced*, v-vi; A. A. Vandegrift and Robert B. Asprey, *Once a Marine* (New York: Norton, 1964), 61; Hough, ibid., 8-10; Moskin, ibid., 459-61; Millett, *Semper*, 325-6; Russell, "Genesis," 19-20; Infusino, ibid., 50-1, 78; Simmons, ibid., 125. Earl H. Ellis has been a mysterious and controversial figure in Marine Corps History. For the most recent reading of his life, see Dirk Anthony Ballendorf, "Earl Hancock Ellis: A Final Assessment," *MCG* 74 (November 1990): 79-87.

20. Earl H. Ellis, *Navy Bases: Their Location, Resources, and Security* (1921; Washington: GPO, 1992), 3-6, 10-23, 30, 48.

21. Iibid., 30, 48.

22. Ellis, *Advanced Base*, 39-50.

23. J. M. Scammell, "Our Naval Bases in the Pacific" *Infantry Journal* 30 (January 1927): 19-29; see also George W. Baer, *One Hundred Years of Sea Power: The U.S. Navy, 1890-1900* (Stanford: Stanford UP, 1994), 91-9; Edward S. Miller, *War Plan Orange: The U.S. Strategy to Defeat Japan, 1897-1945* (Annapolis: Naval Institute, 1991), 83.

24. John A. Lejeune, "The United States Marine Corps," *MCG* 9 (May 1924): 250-3; Rufus H. Lane, "The Mission and Doctrine of the Marine Corps," *MCG* 8 (March 1923): 6-7, 9; Ben H. Fuller, "The Mission of the Marine Corps," *MCG* 15 (November 1930): 7; Raymond O'Connor, "Naval Strategy in the Twentieth Century," *Naval War College Review* 21 (February 1961): 4-10.

25. Lejeune, "United States," 250; Millett, *Semper*, 322-8; Baer, 91-2; Ronald Spector, "The Military Effectiveness of the US Armed Forces, 1919-39," in *Military Effectiveness Volume II: The Interwar Period*, ed. Allan R. Millet and Williamson Murray (Boston: Allen, 1988), 86.

26. HQMC, memo for GB, 11 February 1922, GBSF 1900-1947, GB 432, Box 163, RG 80, NA; memoir of Russell N. Jordahl (1970), MCOHC, 13; Krulak, ibid., 142-3. For

secondary commentary, see Millett, *Semper*, 654; Greene, ibid., 360-1; Spector, *Eagle*, 20-1; Kajiwara, ibid, 6-7; Calvin L. Christman, "Franklin D. Roosevelt and the Craft of Strategic Assessment," *Calculations: Net Assessment and the Coming of World War II*, ed. Williamson Murray and Allan R. Millett (New York: Free Press, 1992), 238; Millett, *Semper*, 320; Philip T. Rosen, "The Treaty Navy, 1919-1937," in *In Peace and War: Interpretations of American Naval History, 1775-1984*, ed. Kenneth J. Hagan (Westport, CN: Greenwood Press 1984).

27. Victor Krulak, *First to Fight: An Inside View of the U.S. Marine Corps* (Annapolis, MD: Naval Institute, 1984), 142; memoir of Charles G. F. Good, Jr. (1970), Marine Corps Oral Historical Center (MCOHC), 90; Russell, ibid., 17; Spector, *Eagle*, 25.

28. "Joint Army and Navy Basic War Plan—ORANGE," 6 October 1920, op. cited in Infusino, ibid., 145.

29. Miller, ibid., 79. The secondary literature on ORANGE is voluminous. For example see, Millett, *Semper*, 320; Spector, *Eagle*, 56-7; Steven T. Ross, ed., *Plans to Meet the Axis Threat, 1939-1940*, vol. 3, *American War Plans* (New York: Garland, 1992), vii; Lester H. Brune, *The Origins of American National Security Policy: Sea Power, Air Power, and Foreign Policy* (Manhattan, KS: MA/HA, 1981), 110-8; Stoler, "Pacific-First," 433; Maurice Matloff and Edwin M. Snell, *United States Army in World War II: Strategy Planning for Coalition Warfare, 1941-2* (Washington: OCMH, 1953), 1-2, 6-9.

30. HQMC, memo for GB, 11 February 1922, GBSF 1900-47, GB 432, Box 163, RG 80, NA; Brune, ibid., 108-9; Morison, ibid., 33.

31. Millett, *Semper*, 328; Weigley, *American*, 255.

32. E. W. Broadbent, "The Fleet and the Marines," *United States Naval Institute Proceedings* 57 (March 1931): 370; GB to Sec Nav, 10 August 1932, "Examination of the Organization and Establishment of the United States Marine Corps," GBSF 1900-1947, GB 432, Box 163, RG 80, NA.

33. Gordon, "Golden," 259; O'Connor, ibid., 8-9; Millett, *Semper*, 319; Kajiwara, ibid., 9; Robert Debs Heinl Jr., *Soldiers of the Sea: The United States Marine Corps, 1775-1962* (Annapolis: Naval Institute, 1962; Baltimore: Nautical and Aviation, 1991), 300-2.

34. Heinl, *Soldiers*, 668-9; Huntington, *Soldier*, 291-3.

35. W. C. Neville, "The Marine Corps," *USNIP* 55 (October 1929): 863; Jack Shulimson, *The Marine Corps' Search for a Mission, 1880-1898* (Lawrence: University of Kansas Press, 1993), 208-9.

36. Broadbent, ibid., 865-6; Allan R. Millett, *In Many a Strife: Gerald C. Thomas and the U.S. Marine Corps, 1917-1956* (Annapolis: Naval Institute. 1993), 98; Cooper, ibid., 104-5. The Army also faced promotion problems during the lean twenties and thirties;

George Marshall advocated a shift to a merit-based program (Larry I. Bland and Sharon R. Ritenour, ed., *The Papers of George Catlett Marshall, vol. 1*, "The Soldierly Spirit," December 1880-June 1939 [Baltimore: Johns Hopkins UP, 1981], 325-6, 348, 390-1, 480).

37. Broadbent, ibid., 369.

38. E. B. Miller, "The Marine Corps: Its Mission, Organization, Power, and Limitation," *MCG* 17 (November 1932): 10-11; Prefer, ibid., 67-72.

39. O'Connor, ibid., 5-10; Russell F. Weigley, "The Interwar Army, 1919-1941," in *Military Effectiveness Volume II: The Interwar Period*, ed. Allan R. Millett and Williamson Murray (Boston: Allen, 1988), 265-6.

40. Broadbent, ibid., 369; Miller, ibid., 10-11, 18; H.C. Pierce, "The New 75-mm Pack Howitzer," *MCG* 15 (March 1930): 31-2.

41. Christman, ibid., 224-5; Kenneth J. Hagan, *This People's Navy: The Making of American Seapower* (New York: Free Press, 1991), 314-5; and Robert William Love, Jr., "Fighting a Global War, 1941-1945," in *In Peace and War: Interpretations of American Naval History*, ed. Kenneth J. Hagan (Westport, CN: Greenwood, 1984), 265; Spector, "Military," 87.

42. Baer, ibid., 120-3.

43. Dion Williams, "The Temporary Defense of a Fleet Base" *MCG* (February 1931): 12; Robert Lindsey, *This High Name: Public Relations and the U.S. Marine Corps* (Madison: University of Wisconsin Press, 1956), 42-4.

44. Spector, "Military," 81; Greene, ibid., 355-77; See also Stetson Conn, "Changing Concepts of National Defense in the United States, 1937-1947," *MA* 28 (Spring 1964): 1-7.

45. Vandegrift, ibid., 90; For the U.S. Army's situation, see Weigley, "Interwar." For a specific explanation of the Monroe Doctrine from approximately the mid-1930s, see F. B. Upshaw, "A Naval View of the Monroe Doctrine," n.d., GBSF 1900-1947, GB 433, Box 163, RG 80, NA.

46. George Fielding Eliot, *The Ramparts We Watch: A Study of the Problems of National Defense* (New York: Reynal and Hitchcock, 1939), 6-7; Hagan, ibid., 281.

47. Brune, ibid., 106. See also Spector, *Eagle*, 21-2; William Emerson, "Franklin Roosevelt as Commander-in-Chief in World War II" *MA* 22 (Winter 1958-9): 181-207; and John Edward Dwan, II, "Franklin Roosevelt and the Revolution in the Strategy of National Security: Foreign Policy and Military Planning Before Pearl Harbor." (Ph.D. diss., Yale University, 1954), 8-11, 128-30.

48. Susan Landrum, "Carl Vinson: A Study in Military Preparedness" (M.A. thesis, Emory University, 1966), 29; Lindsey, ibid., 44.

49. There is a general consensus regarding Roosevelt's popularity with the Navy and the Corps: Mark A. Stoler, "U. S. Civil-Military Relations in World War II," *Parameters* 21 (1991): 61-9; Ernest R. May, "The Development of Political-Military Consultation in the United States," *Political Science Quarterly* 70 (June 1955): 175; Millett, Allan R. Millett, "The American Political System and Civilian Control of the Military: A Historical Perspective," *Mershon Center Position Papers in the Policy Sciences* 4 (April 1979): 23-26; George V. Fagan, "FDR and Naval Limitations," *USNIP* 81 (April 1955): 414; Emerson, ibid., 181-3.

50. Memoir of Clifton B. Gates (1969), MCOHC, 97; Senator Phillip Lee Goldsborough to Estell Smith Kepler, 3 February 1933, Julian C. Smith Papers, Marine Corps Personal Papers Collection (MCPPC), Box 28, Marine Corps Historical Center (MCHC). See also, John C. Walter, "Congressman Carl Vinson and Franklin D. Roosevelt: Naval Preparedness and the Coming of World War II, 1939-1940," *Georgia Historical Quarterly* 64 (Fall 1980): 294, 298, 305; Julius Augustus, *Administration of the Navy Department in World War II* (Washington: GPO, 1959), 47-50; Hagan, ibid., 281-7, 294.

51. "Biography," MGC to Melvin J. Maas, 12 January 1933, both in Melvin J. Maas File, Reference Section, MCHC; Heinl, *Soldiers*, 297.

52. Marshall to John L. De Witt, 16 October 1933, *Marshall Papers*, vol. 1, 401; Vandegrift, ibid., 89-90; Gordon, "Golden," 261-2; Samuel P. Huntington, "Interservice Competition and Political Roles of the Armed Services," in *Total War and Cold War*, ed. Harry L. Coles (Columbus: OSUP, 1962), 180-5; Millett, *Semper*, 628.

53. MGC to CNO, "Expeditionary Force," 17 August 1933, and MGC to L. McCarty Little, "Fleet Marine Force," 5 December 1933, both in File 1975-10, Personnel Department General Correspondence (PDGC), 1933-1938, Box 135, RG 127, NA. See also Russell, "Birth," 49-51; Millett, *Semper*, 330-7; W. H. Russell, ibid., 22; Prefer, ibid., 157-8; Hough, ibid., 11-4; Heinl, *Soldiers*, 299-305; Infusino, ibid., 84-93; Metcalf, ibid., 550-1.

54. Memoirs of William J. Van Ryzin (1975), MCOHC, 74-6; Ryzin eventually joined the First Defense Battalion. In addition, a consensus of historians concur that the Marine Corps highlighted the island defense component of the FMF's mission for purposes public relations. For example, Millett, *Semper*, 319; Isely, ibid., 74-5; Heinl, *Soldiers*, 306; Spector, *Eagle*, 27; Kajiwara, ibid., 11.

55. Heinl, *Soldiers*, 315; Spector, "Military," 84-6; Clifford, ibid., 58-9; Robert Sherrod, *History of Marine Corps Aviation in World War II* (Washington, Combined Force Press, 1952), 30-33.

56. Kenneth J. Clifford, *Progress and Purpose: A Developmental History of the United States Marine Corps 1900-1970* (Washington: USMC, 1973), 45-8; Isley, ibid., 5; Weigley, *American*, 255-7; Millett, *Semper*, 319, 331-3; Heinl, *Soldiers*, 300-2.

57. Marine Corps Schools, *Tentative Manual of Landing Operations*, 1934, Marine Corps Historical Library (MCHL), MCHC, paragraph 1-1, 1-2, 1-5, 1-8, 1-22, 3-120; Krulak, ibid., 81-2; John Breckenridge, "Some Thoughts on Policy, Strategy, and Comparative Power" and "A Discussion of Power," 21 November 1934, Julian C. Smith Papers, MCPPC, Box 29, MCHC. For further commentary, see also, Isley, ibid., 36-44; Clifford, ibid., 46-8; Hough, ibid., 14-22; Millett, *Semper*, 331-7, 343; Millett, *In Many*, 110-5; Spector, "Military," 84-5.

58. Weigley, "Interwar," 258-62; see also Kajiwara, ibid., 21-6.

59. Memoirs of Thomas E. Bourke (1969), MCOHC, 19. Promotion bottlenecks were not limited to the Corps and the Navy. According to George Marshall, the promotion bottleneck also affected the Army during the Depression years (Marshall to Philip E. Gallagher, 27 September 1932, Marshall to Edgar T. Collins, 30 September 1932; John J. Pershing to Marshall, 20 December 1935, all in *Marshall Papers*, vol. 1, 379-81, 479-80).

60. Memoir of Oliver P. Smith (1969), MCOHC, 78-9; memoir of Samuel B. Griffith II (1968), MCOHC, 30-1; Smith, *Thomas*, 1-2; "Portraits of the Commandants," *MCG* 59 (November 1975): 31-97; Gordon, "Golden," 256-61; Millett, *Semper*, 325. With the exception of a chapter on Holcomb by Gordon in Millett's forthcoming anthology on Commandants, this article is the only lengthy treatment of Holcomb.

61. Memoir of Robert H. Williams (1979, 1980), MCOHC, 65-6; memoir of Oliver P. Smith (1969), MCOHC, 79; Lyman to Alexander A. Vandegrift, 22 July 1938, Alexander A. Vandegrift Papers, MCPPC, Box 2, MCHC.

62. See author's questionnaire with responses from 80 Marines veterans of the 7th Defense Battalion. 31 of 80 surveyed Marines responded to the following question "What role (1936-43) did Commandant Thomas Holcomb play in the development of the Marine Corps in general and the defense battalion in particular? Was he an administrator, strategist, salesman, etc.?" Those who did not respond to this question claimed either they joined too late to know anything of Holcomb or their ranks were too low to have any knowledge of Holcomb's role as Commandant.

63. Millett, *Semper*, 334-41; Cameron, ibid., 27; Kenneth W. Condit, et.al, *A Brief History of Headquarters Marine Corps Staff Organization*, rev. (Washington: USMC, 1970), 15; Gordon, "General," 256-60, 269; Heinl, *Soldiers*, 306; Furer, ibid. 551-3.

64. Lyman to Vandegrift, 22 July 1938, Vandegrift Papers, MCPPC, Box 2, MCHC; Cameron, ibid., 43-5; Gordon, "Golden," 263; Lindsey, ibid., 48-9.

65. Thomas Holcomb, speech, "The Contribution of the Marine Corps the National Defense," 27 January 1927, Thomas Holcomb File, Reference Section, MCHC. For

another example of Marine self-promotion, see Clayton B. Vogel, speech, "The Marines and Our First Line of Defense," October 1938, Vandegrift Papers, MCPPC, Box 2, MCHC; Millett, *Semper*, 336. The U.S. Army also endeavored to gain appropriations publicizing itself. In speech to the West Virginia American Legion Convention on 4 September 1938, George Marshall makes a similar appeal for support of national defense (*Marshall Papers*, vol. 1, 620-5).

66. Holcomb to D.C. McDougal, 7 March 1937, Holcomb Papers, MCPPC, Box 1, MCHC. For examples of Lejeune's lobbying, see Lejeune to Holcomb, 24 January 1938, and Lejeune to Holcomb, 20 April 1938, both in Holcomb Papers, MCPPC, Box 2, MCHC; George Killen, survey questionnaire, 1995.

67. McDougal to Vandegrift, 22 July 1938, Vandegrift Papers, MCPPC, Box 2, MCHC. Holcomb's correspondence which evaluates the 1938 Personnel Bill includes the following: Lejeune to Holcomb, 24 January 1938, Holcomb to Richard P. Williams, 2 March 1938, Holcomb to Gilder Jackson, 7 April 1938, Lejeune to Holcomb, 20 April 1938, Holcomb to John C. Beaumont, 27 April 1938, Holcomb to David I. Walsh, 9 June 1938, Holcomb to McDougal, 15 June 1938, Thomas Holcomb to Lyman, 30 June 1938, all in Holcomb Papers, MCPPC, Box 2, MCHC.

68. Calvin William Enders, "The Vinson Navy" (Ph.D. diss., Michigan State University, 1970), 116-20; Landrum, ibid., 57-9, 79; Walters, ibid., 301-2.

69. Statutory Board on Submarine, Mine, and Naval Bases, 1938, memo for Secretary of the Navy, 1 December 1938, World War II Command File, Operational Archives, Box 63, Naval Historical Center (NHC); Holcomb, letter to Harry K. Pickett, 12 December 1938, Accession Number (AN) 127-77-30, Box 2, National Records Center (NRC); Louis Morton, "Interservice Co-operation and Political-Military Collaboration," in *Total War and Cold War* ed. Harry L. Coles (Columbus: OSUP, 1962), 153; Morison, ibid., 32-4; Spector, "Military," 74; Metcalf, 554-5; Matloff, *United*, 3.

70. Holcomb, letter to D. C. McDougal, 25 May 1937; John H. Russell, letter to Holcomb, 11 October 1937; Diek, letter to Holcomb, 19 February 1938; all in Thomas Holcomb Papers, MCPPC, Box 1, MCHC; Thomas Holcomb to Harry K. Pickett, "Obtaining information in regard to certain United States Possessions in the Pacific Ocean," 12 December 1938, AN 127-77-30, Box 1, NRC; memoir of William W. Buchanan (1969), MCOHC, 12-4; Charles L. Updegraph, Jr., *U.S. Marine Corps Special Units of World War II* (Washington: USMC, 1977), 61-2; Millett, *Semper*, 343-5; Infusino, ibid., 90-2.

71. Brune, ibid., 108-11; Ross, ibid., x-xii; Stetson Conn, "Changing Concepts of National Defense in the United States, 1937-1947," *MA* 28 (Spring 1964): 1-7; Baer, ibid., 146, 152.

72. Infusino, ibid., 108; Kajiwara, ibid., 12-4; Furer, ibid., 560; Matloff, ibid., 6-10. O'Connor, ibid., 8-9.

73. Memoir of William W. Buchanan, (1969) MCOHC, 38; memoir of Russell N Jordahl (1970), 78; memoir of Samuel G. Taxis (1981), 40-4; memoir of Henry R. Paige (1970), 37-8; James A. Donovan, Jr., *The United States Marine Corps* (New York: Praeger, 1967), 74-8; Isley, ibid, 74-5; Heinl, *Soldiers*, 305-307; Millett, *Semper*, 268-9, 344-5; Melson, ibid., 4-5.

74. Robert F. Cyperski, Salvatore J. Butta, Antonio Santaniell, Charles H. Petersen, all in Survey Questionnaires.

CHAPTER 2 NOTES

1. Maurice Matloff, "Prewar Military Plans and Preparations: 1939-1940" *USNIP* 79 (July 1953): 741-2; Huntington, "Interservice," 180; Millett, *For the Common Defense*, 388; Fagan, ibid., 411.

2. Vandegrift, ibid., 86-9; 11 Feb 1939, JCF to Holcomb, 8 March 1939, Holcomb to A. S. Carpender, 9 March 1939, 12 January 1940, Holcomb to Clifton Woodrum, all in Holcomb Papers, MCPPC, Box 3 and 4, MCHC.

3. CNO to Department Chiefs, 16 Feb 1939, Division of Plans and Policies, War Plans Section, General Correspondence (DPPWPSGC) 1926-42, Box 4, RG 127, NA; JCF to Holcomb, 11 Feb 1939, Holcomb Papers, MCPPC, Box 3, MCHC; Eliot, ibid., 161-76, 234; Frederick J. Nelson, "Guam—Our Western Outpost," *USNIP* 66 (January 1940): 83-8. Millett, *Many*, 130-2; Hough, ibid., 59-62; Spector, *Eagle*, 40-5; Major, ibid., 243-5; D. Clayton James, "American and Japanese Strategies in the Pacific War," *Makers of Modern Strategy from Machiavelli to the Nuclear Age*, ed. Peter Paret (Princeton: Princeton UP, 1986), 706-7.

4. For an overview of the RAINBOW plans, see Matloff, *United*, 4-Kajiwara, ibid., 13; Infusino, ibid., 94-6, 108; Dwan, ibid., 56-5; Greene, ibid., 374-5.

5. J. B. Earle, memo for the CNO, 8 September 1939, SecNav to SecWar, 29 September 1939, both in DPPWPSGC 1926-42, Box 4, RG 127, NA; Updegraph, ibid., 62-3.

6. Holcomb to Commanding General FMF, 28 March 1939, DPPWPSGC 1926-42, Box 4, RG 127, NA; Holcomb to A. W. Johnson, 27 April 1939, Holcomb Papers, MCPPC, Box 3, MCHC. For a study of Marine Reserve, see Reserve Officers of Public Affairs Unit 4-1, *The Marine Corps Reserve: A History* (Washington, DC: MCHQ, 1966).

7. Chairman, GB to SecNav, memo, "Are We Ready?" 31 August 1939, File 425, GB Records, RG 80, NARA cited in Millett, *Semper*, 342; "The Defense of Wake" and "The Defense of Palmyra," 11 August 1939, DPPWPSGC 1921-43, Box 34, RG 127, NA; memoir of Lester A. Dessez (1970), 157, MCOHC; memoir, Taxis, 53; See also Miller, ibid., 241-3. For a brief biography of Stark, see B. Mitchell Simpson, III,

"Harold Raynsford Stark, 1 August 1939 to 26 March 1942," *Chiefs of Naval Operations*, ed. Robert W. Love, Jr. (Annapolis: Naval Institute, 1980).

8. Stark, memo for Holcomb, 7 August 1939, Marshall to President Roosevelt, 11 August 1939, George V. Strong to Marshall, 11 August 1939, all in DPPWPSGC 1926-42, Box 4, RG 127, NA; memoir, Paige, 37-8; Carolyn A. Tyson, A Chronology of the United States Marine Corps, 1936-1946, Volume 2 (Washington: USMC, 1977), 7.

9. Marshall, memo for Stark, August 18, 1939, DPPWPSGC 1926-42, Box 4, RG 127, NA.

10. Miller, ibid., 242-3.

11. Memo, 15 August 1939, Holcomb to Stark, August 17, 1939, both in DPPWPSGC 1926-42, Box 4, RG 127, NA; Eliot, ibid., 230-1; Heinl, *Soldiers*, 306-7.

12. Henry A. Larsen, memo for Holcomb, 12 Oct 1939, DPPWPSGC 1926-42, Box 4, RG 127, NA; Furer, ibid., 41-2, 560-1; Vandegrift, ibid., 92-4; Millett, *Semper*, 345; Millet, *Many*, 132-3.

13. Secretary of War to Secretary of the Navy, 9 October 1939, Larsen to Holcomb, 12 October 1939, both in DPPWPSGC 1926-42, Box 4, RG 127, NA; "the Defense of Midway," DPPWPSGC 1921-43, Box 33, RG 127, NA.

14. Robert L. Denig to Holcomb, 26 Oct 1939, Holcomb Papers, MCPPC, Box 3, MCHC. The Army was in a similar situation; see Weigley, *History*, 423-30.

15. Lindsey, ibid., 49; Vandegrift, ibid., 91.

16. Holcomb to Vandegrift, 22 March 1939, Holcomb to Denig, 6 Nov 1939, both in Holcomb Papers, MCPPC, Box 3, MCHC; Alan Brown to Campbell, 12 Oct 1939, Vandegrift to Brown, 28 Oct 1939, Vandegrift to Leo D. Hermle, 13 Nov 1939, all in Vandegrift Papers, MCPPC, Box 2, MCHC; *Marine Corps Administrative History*, typed manuscript (Washington: Marine Corps Historical Division, 1946), (*MCAH*), 8-9; Gordon, "Golden," 263; Vandegrift, ibid., 91.

17. Updegraph, ibid., 64; Holcomb to Denig, 6 Nov 1939, Holcomb Papers, MCPPC, Box 3, MCHC; Vandegrift to Gilder D. Jackson, 10 July 1940, Vandegrift Papers, MCPPC, Box 2, MCHC.

18. P. A. del Valle, memo for Holcomb, 22 Dec 1939, DPPWPSGC 1915-46, Box 14, RG 127, NA; memoir of James P. S. Devereux (1970), MCOHC, 92-3; memoir, Taxis, 40-58. For secondary commentary, see Infusino, ibid., 99-101; Kajiwara, ibid., 15-6; Hough, ibid., 49. For basic studies of Wake, see Millet, *Semper*. 355-6; Hough, ibid., 108-14.

19. Mark W. Lowenthal, "The Stark Memorandum and the American National Security Process, 1940," in *Changing Interpretations and New Sources in Naval History*, ed Robert W. Love, Jr. (New York: Garland, 1980), 354-5; Kimmel to Thomas Hart, 9 February 1940, "Reflections of the Far Eastern Situation and Certain Problems of U.S. Far Eastern Policy," 4 July 1940, Stanley to Sumner Welles, 21 September 1940, all in *Hearings before the Joint Committee on the Investigation of the Pearl Harbor Attack*, 79th Congress, 1st Session, GPO 1946 (*Hearings*), 2444-48; Hagan, 292; Weigley, *History*, 426-9.

20. Clifford, ibid., 61; Millett, *Semper*, 345; see Appendices 3 and 5.

21. Stoler, "U.S.-Military," 62, Spector, "Military," 77; Vandegrift to Hermle, 13 Nov 1939, Vandegrift Papers, MCPPC, Box 2, MCHC.

22. *MCAH*, ibid., 1-11b; Furer, ibid., 551-55.

23. Vandegrift, ibid., 88.

24. Dr. Phyllis A. Zimmerman, associate professor of military history at Ball State University, likens a Commandant's role to that of a college president.

25. Julius Augustus Furer, *Administration of the Navy Department in World War II* (Washington: GPO, 1959), 551. Regarding the Assistant to the Commandant's duties, see Vandegrift to Roice L. Biffle, 11 March 1940, Vandegrift Papers, MCPPC, Box 2, MCHC. This was part of a petition filed by a sergeant denied promotion; it was directed to Assistant Vandegrift.

26. William Upshur to Holcomb, 25 April 1940, Holcomb Papers, MCPPC, Box 4, MCHC; letter to Vandegrift, 22 August 1940, Vandegrift Papers, MCPPC, Box 2, MCHC.

27. Holcomb to Upshur, 12 July 1940, Holcomb to George F. Eliot, 17 July 1940, Holcomb to Eliot, 24 July 1940, Holcomb to Vinson, 24 July 1940, Eliot to Holcomb, 17 August 1940, all in Holcomb Papers, MCPPC, Box 4, MCHC; Vandegrift to Holcomb, 15 July 1940, Vandegrift Papers, MCPPC, Box 2, MCHC; Millett, *Semper*, 347.

28. Vandegrift to Biffle, 11 March 1940, Lloyd to Vandegrift, 2 August 1940, both in Vandegrift Papers, MCPPC, Box 2, MCHC; Upshur to Holcomb, 25 April 1940, Holcomb to Vinson, 24 July 1940, both in Holcomb Papers, MCPPC, Box 4, MCHC; Cameron, ibid., 56-9; Millett, *Semper*, 348-49; Heinl, *Soldiers*, 315, Millett, *Many*, 134. For a discussion of the promotion stagnation during Lejeune's Commandancy, see memoir of Russell N. Jordahl (1970), MCOHC, 13; Krulak, ibid., 142-3; Millet, *Semper*, 322-4.

29. Holcomb, memo for Eliot, 24 July 1940, Holcomb Papers, MCPPC, Box 4, MCHC; 8 August 1940, Vandegrift Papers, MCPPC, Box 2, MCHC; E. B. Sledge, *With the Old Breed* (Novato: Presidio Press, 1981), chapter 1; Millett, *Semper*, 347-8; Salvatore J.

Butta, Robert F. Cyperski, R. B. Dunkleberger, A. G. Smith Jr., Robert L. High, William McGuire, Steven Kiraly, Truxton Ringe, Odell C. Reid, Donald J. Brisbois, Edward J. Dieckmann, all in Survey Questionnaire.

30. John Marston to Vandegrift, 21 June 1940, Vandegrift Papers, MCPPC, Box 2, MCHC; Heinl, *Soldiers*, 315-7; Millet, *Many*, 15-6.

31. Vandegrift to Marston, 29 June 1940, Vandegrift Papers, MCPPC, Box 2, MCHC; Heinl, *Soldiers*, 307.

32. Millett, *Many*, 134-6; Heinl, *Soldiers*, 305; Simmons, ibid., 138.

33. Memo for Holcomb, 16 June 1940, DPPWPSWP 1915-46, Box 14, RG 127, NA; Vandegrift to Marston, 29 June 1940, Vandegrift Papers, MCPPC, Box 2, MCHC.

34. Millett, *Semper*, 351-2.

35. 4 July 1940, *Hearings*, 1989-97; Heinl, *Soldiers*, 310-11; Miller, ibid., 243; Millett, *Semper*, 345; Major, ibid., 258-9; James, ibid., 709; July 16, 1940, "Reflections on certain features of the Far Eastern situation and certain problems of U.S. Far Eastern policy, July 4, 1940," *Hearings*, 1989-97. For further explanation, see James H. Herzog, "Influence of the United States Navy in the Embargo of Oil to Japan" *Pacific Historical Review* 35 (August 1966): 317-28.

36. Vandegrift to Leech, 8 July 1940, Vandegrift to Jackson, 10 July 1940, both in Vandegrift Papers, MCPPC, Box 2, MCHC; memoir, Loomis, 98-9.

37. Eliot to Holcomb, 17 August 1940, Holcomb, memo for Eliot, 24 July 1940, both in Holcomb Papers, MCPPC, Box 4, MCHC; letter to Vandegrift, 22 August 1940, Vandegrift Papers, MCPPC, Box 2, MCHC; Kajiwara, ibid., 14.

38. Memoirs, Van Ryzin, 74; 6 November 1940, Holcomb to All Officers, Charles Melson's Personal Library. For an earlier version of Heinl's article see 15 August 1939, "Defense Battalions," DPPWPSGC 1926-42, Box 4, RG 127, NA.

39. 6 November 1940, Holcomb to All Officers, Charles Melson's Personal Library.

40. Ibid.

41. 6 November 1940, Holcomb to All Officers, Charles Melson's Personal Library; Heinl, *Soldiers*, 310-11; 8 July 1940, 10 July 1940, both in Vandegrift Papers, MCPPC, Box 2, MCHC; Miller, ibid., 243.

42. *Hearings*, 2448-9; Millett, *Semper*, 397; Lowenthal, ibid., 355.

43. Gordon, "Golden," 263-4.

44. Holcomb to Otis Swift, 29 October 1940, Daniel Longwell to Holcomb, 12 November 1940, Otis Swift to Holcomb, 13 November 1940, Holcomb to Longwell, 14 November, 1940, Longwell to Holcomb, 25 November 1940, all in Holcomb PPC, Box 4.

45. "National Defense," *Time* 36.20 11 November 1940, 21-3; Crosby Maynard to Holcomb, 6 November 1940; Sam Meek to Holcomb, 8 November 1940; Holcomb to Meek, 12 November 1940; Holcomb to Henry R. Luce, 12 November 1940; Meek to Holcomb, 15 November 1940; Luce to Holcomb, 15 November 1940; Holcomb to James G. Harbord, 12 November 1940; all in Holcomb PPC, Box 4. See also Gordon, "Golden," 263-5; and Cameron, ibid., 49-88.

CHAPTER 3 NOTES

1. CNO to CINCPAC, CINCLANT, and CINCASIA, April 3, 1941, *Hearings*, 2462-3.

2. Lowenthal, ibid., 352-61; Ross, ibid., xiv.

3. Ross, ibid., 244-8; Lowenthal, ibid., 355-7; Infusino, ibid., 96.

4. Ernest J. King, *U.S. Navy at War 1941-1945: Official Reports to the Secretary of the Navy* (Washington: Navy Dept, 1946), 37. For the most part, the whole military believed that a war with Japan would inevitably occur.

5. Woodrow Kessler, *To Wake and Beyond: Reminiscences* (Washington: USMC, 1988), 15; see also Joan E. Sparks (Mrs. Ernest W. Sparks), James Martin Callender, George Killen, Maurice Gremillion, Survey Questionnaire; Baer, ibid., 177-8; Melson, ibid, 1-3, 5-6.

6. "Plan DOG," op. cited in Ross, ibid., 227-9; Lowenthal, ibid., 258-9; Morison, ibid., 49-51; James, ibid, 711; Brune, ibid., 116.

7. "ABC-1 Annex 3," 27 March 1941, *Hearings*, 1504, 1511-3; CNO to CINCPAC, CINCLANT, and CINCAF, April 3, 1941, *Hearings*, 2462-3. Numerous secondary sources include James, ibid, 711; Brune, ibid., 116-7; Millett, *Common*, 397-8; Infusino, ibid., 97-8; Major, ibid, 255-6; Morison, ibid., 49-53, 184; Hough, ibid., 64; Updegraph, ibid., 65.

8. "ABC-1 Annex 3," 27 March 1941, *Hearings*, 1511-2.

9. Ingersoll to Holcomb, 10 January 1941, DPPWPSGC 1926-42, Box 4, RG 127, NA.

10. Stark to Director of Ship Movement Division, 17 January 1941, Stark to Kimmel, 26 February 1941, both in AN 1277-77-30, Box 2, NRC.

11. Kimmel to Stark, 11 February 1941, Kimmel to Stark, 18 February 1941, Ingersoll to Kimmel, 19 February 1941, all in AN 1277-77-30, Box 2, NRC; Ingersoll to Holcomb, 10 January 1941, DPPWPSGC 1926-42, Box 4, RG 127, NA; Holcomb to J. W. Greenslade, 30 January 1941, GBSF 1900-47, GB 432, Box 163, RG 80, NA; Bureau of Yards and Dock, 1 March 1941, GBSF 1900-47, GB 425, Box 135, RG 80, NA.

12. For, the third conclusion, see CNO to CINCPAC, CINCLANT, and CINCASIA, April 3, 1941, *Hearings*, 2462-3; James H. Reid to Stark, 2 February 1941, A. G. Kirk to Stark, 20 February 1941, both in GBSF 1900-47, General Correspondence of CNO and SecNav (GCCNOSN), Box 54, RG 80, NA; Kimmel to Stark, 18 February 1941, AN 127-77-30, Box 1, NRC; Homer C. Votaw, "Wake Island," *USNIP* 67 (January 1941): 52-5; Infusino, 96; Millett, *Common*, 398.

13. M. E. Shearer to Vandegrift, 29 January 1941, Vandegrift Papers, PPC, Box 2, MCHC; Holcomb to Stark, 9 January 1941, Holcomb to Vinson, 9 January 1941, Holcomb to Charles C. Long, 30 January 1941, all in Holcomb Papers, PPC, Box 5, MCHC; Charles H. Petersen, Survey Questionnaire; Millett, *Semper*, 346-9.

14. "Marine Expeditionary Force," n.d. [28 February 1941], "Training Units of the Fleet Marine Force," n.d. [1 March 1941], both in GBSF 1900-47, GB 425, Box 135, RG 80, NA; Ingersoll to Department Chiefs, 28 February 1941, AN 1277-77-30, Box 2, NRC; see also Melson, ibid., 4-6.

15. "Marine Expeditionary Force," n.d. [28 February 1941], "Training Units of the Fleet Marine Force," n.d. [1 March 1941], both in GBSF 1900-47, GB 425, Box 135, RG 80, NA; Ingersoll to Department Chiefs, 28 February 1941, AN 1277-77-30, Box 2, NRC.

16. CNO to CINCPAC, CINCLANT, CINCAF, 3 April 1941, *Hearings*, 2462-3; Breckenridge to Vandegrift, 2 April 1941, Vandegrift to Marston, 21 April 1941, Price to Vandegrift, 8 May, all in Vandegrift Papers, PPC, Box 2, MCHC; MGC, Memo for CNO, 2 June 1941, Chief of the Bureau of Ordnance, memo for SecNav, 3 June 1941, GCCNOSN, 1940-7, Box 51, RG 80, NA; Infusino, 97-100, 108; Millett, *Common*, 398.

17. Vandergrift to Denig, 4 March 1941, Vandegrift Papers, PPC, Box 2, MCHC; CNO to MGC, 29 April 1941, DPPWPSGS 1926-42, Box 4, RG 127, NA.

18. Kimmel to Chester W. Nimitz, 2 Feb 1941, *Hearings*, 2460; Vandegrift to Price, 11 March 1941, Price to Vandegrift, 9 April 1941, both in Vandegrift Papers, PPC, Box 2, MCHC.

19. Breckinridge to Vandegrift, 2 April 1941, Price to Vandegrift, 9 April 1941, Price to Vandegrift, 8 May 1941, all in Vandegrift Papers, PPC, Box 2, MCHC.

20. Vandegrift to Denig, 4 March 1941, Vandegrift to Lyman, 6 March 1941, Vandegrift to Price, 11 March 1941, Vandegrift to Dave [?], 21 August 1941, Vandegrift to

Marston, 25 August 1941, all in Vandegrift Papers, PPCC, Box 2, MCHC; Antonio Santaniell, Raymond L. Valente, both in Survey Questionnaire.

21. Holcomb to Smith, 10 March 1941, Holcomb Papers, PPC, Box 5, MCHC; see also Lindsay, ibid., 45-53.

22. Holcomb to J.G. Harbord, 17 June 1941, Lawrence [?] to Holcomb, 18 June 1941, Harbord to Holcomb, 18 June 1941, Meek to Holcomb, 24 June 1941, all in Holcomb Papers, PPC, Box 5, MCHC; Gordon, "Golden," 263; Cameron, ibid., 48.

23. Holcomb to Smith, 10 March 1941, Meek to Holcomb, 24 June 1941, both in Holcomb Papers, PPC, Box 5, MCHC.

24. Lindsay, ibid., 50.

25. op. cited in ibid., 50.

26. Condit, ibid., 15-8; Lindsay, ibid., 50-1.

27. Chairman, GB, to SecNav, 7 May 1941, GBSF 1900-1947, GB 432, Box 163, RG 80, NA; Price to Vandegrift, 8 May 1941, Vandegrift to Price, both in Vandegrift Papers, PPC, Box 2, MCHC; Infusino, 104-5; Condit, 15-7.

28. Chairman, GB, to SecNav, 7 May 1941, GBSF 1900-1947, GB 432, Box 163, RG 80, NA; Price to Vandegrift, 8 May 1941, Vandegrift Papers, PPC, Box 2, MCHC.

29. Price to Vandegrift, 8 May 1941, Vandegrift Papers, PPC, Box 2, MCHC.

30. Ibid.

31. It is noteworthy that some of the surveyed leathernecks made multiple responses. For instance, a given respondent might have cited both patriotism and employment as reasons for his becoming a Marine. While such irregularity negates scientific conclusions, the survey does indicate that service as a Marine satisfied recruits' reasons for enlistment. Consequently, the Corps' public image or, to use Craig M. Cameron's word, "myth" would have implicitly helped shape their expectations. See Robert L. High, et. al., all in Survey Questionnaire. In my survey, the reasons for enlistment in the Corps were even more conspicuous. Patriotism, Duty, and Proof of Manhood comprised 25 of 28 responses. Employment shrank to only three responses. Obviously, then, young men chose the Corps over a number of alternatives, all in Survey Questionnaire. For further explanation, see also Cameron, ibid., 21-88; and John W. Gordon, "The U.S. Marine Corps and an Experiment in Military Elitism: A Reassessment of the Special Warfare Impetus, 1937-1943," *Changing Interpretations and New Sources in Naval History*, ed. Robert William Love, Jr. (New York: Garland, 1980), 362-73.

32. Millett, *Many*, 138-9; Hough, ibid., 97-100.

33. CNO to MGC, 29 April 1941, DPPWPSGC, 1926-1942, Box 4, RG 127, NA; Chairman, GB, to SecNav, 7 May 1941, GBSF 1900-1947, GB 432, Box 163, RG 80, NA; *MCAH*, 12.

34. Chairman, GB, to SecNav, 7 May 1941, GBSF 1900-1947, GB 432, Box 163, RG 80, NA.

35. CNO to CINCPAC, 6 May 1941, AN 127-77-30, Box 1, NRC; memo, "Defense of Bases Established for the Support of the Fleet," 13 May 1941, DPPWPSGC 1926-42, Box 1, RG 127, NA; Chairman, GB, to SecNav, 7 May 1941, GBSF 1900-1947, GB 432, Box 163, RG 80, NA; memoir, Pfeiffer, 130-1; Edward T. Peniston, Survey Questionnaire; Kajiwara, ibid., 22-3, 27-8.

36. Memo, "Defense of Bases Established for the Support of the Fleet," 13 May 1941, DPPWPSGC 1926-42, Box 1, RG 127, NA; Chairman, GB, to SecNav, 7 May 1941, GBSF 1900-1947, GB 432, Box 163, RG 80, NA; Millett, *Semper*, 346-7; see also Updegraph.

37. CNO to MGC, 29 April 1941, CNO to MGC, 12 May 1941, both in DPPWPSGC, 1926-42, Box 4, RG 127, NA; Memo, "Defense of Bases Established for the Support of the Fleet," 13 May 1941, DPPWPSGC 1926-42, Box 1, RG 127, NA; CINCPAC to CNO, 28 May 1941, AN 127-77-30, Box 2, NRC.

38. Memo, "Defense of Bases Established for the Support of the Fleet," 13 May 1941, DPPWPSGC 1926-42, Box 1, RG 127, NA; Stark to Marshall, 22 May 1941, DPPWPSGC 1926-42, Box 1, RG 127, NA; Chief of Bureau of Ordnance, 2 June 1941, GCCNOSN 1940-7, Box 51, RG 80, NA; "Are We Ready III - Additional data on Defense Battalions covering period 1 March 1941 to 15 September 1941," 16 September 1941, DPPWPSGC 1940-1, Box 15, RG 127, NA; E. J. Deickmann, Survey Questionnaire; Infusino, 106. For a study of the Army's anti-aircraft artillery situation in the late 1930s and early 1940s, see Bryon W. Greenwald, "The Development of Antiaircraft Artillery Organization, Doctrine, and Technology in the United States Army, 1919-1941" (M.A. thesis, Ohio State University, 1991), 114-8.

39. Ingersoll to Holcomb, 10 January 1941, DPPWPSGC 1926-42, Box 4, RG 127, NA; Jean P. Kirsh, R.B. Dunkleberger, John Volentine, Charles H. Petersen, George B. Bell, William H. Raquet, Otis R. Strong, Antonio Santaniell, Edward H. Walker, Jack N. Murray, Nicholas Sutton, Raymond L. Valente, Truxton Ringe, Denton G. Moulton, Franklin S. Ruhl, Odell C. Reid, John H. Wilson, Walter J. Kerr, Harry Calcutt, Kenneth Patrick, all Survey Questionnaire. Wake also lacked radar among other things (see memoir, Devereux, 104-5).

40. Walter C. Coleman, Otis R. Strong, Franklin S. Ruhl, E. J. Deickmann, Edward T. Peniston, all in Survey Questionnaire.

41. Holcomb to Smith, 10 March 1941, Holcomb Papers, PPC, Box 5, MCHC; Salvatore J. Butta, Robert F. Cyperski, R. B. Dunkleberger, A. G. Smith Jr., Robert L. High, William McGuire, Steven Kiraly, Truxton Ringe, Odell C. Reid, Donald J. Brisbois,

Edward J. Dieckmann, all in Survey Questionnaire; only Walter F. Stanley felt the poor equipment and lack of manpower had a "bad effect on morale," (Survey Questionnaire); Hough, ibid., 66; Cameron, ibid., 36.

42. Holcomb to Smith, 10 March 1941, Holcomb Papers, PPC, Box 5, MCHC; Breckenridge to Vandegrift, 2 April 1941, Vandegrift, memo for F.E. Beatty, 15 July 1941, Vandegrift to Marston, 25 August 1941, all in Vandegrift Papers, PPC, Box 2, MCHC; Vandegrift, ibid., 95-7; Millett, *Many*, 151.

43. Kimmel to Stark, 26 July 1941, *Hearings*, 2239-42; Major, ibid., 258-60; Millett, *Common*, 398-9; James, ibid., 712-4; Millett, *Many*, 150.

44. Major, ibid., 259; Herzog, ibid., 317-28.

45. "U.S. Pacific Fleet Operating Plan - Rainbow Five (Navy 0-1, Rainbow Five)," 21 July 1941, *Hearings*, 2569-88; Infusino. ibid., 102.

46. "U.S. Pacific Fleet Operating Plan - Rainbow Five (Navy 0-1, Rainbow Five)," 21 July 1941, *Hearings*, 2569-88.

47. Voluminous secondary material is available on pre-war strategies and war plans. For example, see Updegraph, ibid., 61-2; Millett, *Semper*, 343-5; Greene, 374-5; Infusino, ibid., 90-6, 108; Kajiwara, ibid., 12-4; Furer, ibid., 560; O'Connor, ibid., 8-9; Maurice Matloff, "Prewar Military Plans and Preparations: 1939-1940" *USNIP* 79 (July 1953): 741-2; Huntington, "Interservice," 180; Fagan, ibid., 411; Lowenthal, ibid., 355-7; Infusino, ibid., 96.

48. Holcomb to CNO, 3 June 1941, GCCNOSN 1940-7, Box 51, RG 80, NA; 23 June 1941; Hough, ibid., 68-9. These sources corroborate the recollections from the Marines in the 7th Defense Battalion. According to Truxton Ringe, the 7th eventually "did not get 90 mm AA guns with microwave radar and more modern seacoast artillery until 1944-5" (Survey Questionnaire). See also Harry Calcutt, Denton G. Moulton, both in Survey Questionnaire.

49. "Are We Ready III - additional data covering period 1 March 1941 to 15 September 1941," 16 September 1941, DPPWPSGC 1940-1, Box 15, RG 127, NA.

50. Vandegrift to Price, 13 September 1941, Vandegrift Papers, PPC, Box 2, MCHC; "Are We Ready III - additional data covering period 1 March 1941 to 15 September 1941," 16 September 1941, DPPWPSGC 1940-1, Box 15, RG 127, NA.

51. "Are We Ready III - Additional data covering period 1 March 1941 to 15 September 1941," 16 September 1941, "Are We Ready III - Additional data on Defense Battalions covering period 1 March 1941 to 15 September 1941," 16 September, both in DPPWPSGC 1940-1, Box 15, RG 127, NA; Holcomb, memo for CNO, 3 June 1941, GCCNOSN 1940-7, Box 51, RG 80, NA; Kimmel to Stark, 12 August 1941, *Hearings*, 2243-5; 12 August, Vandegrift Papers, PPC, MCHC; "Rough draft for

Kimmel's letter," August 16, 1941, *Hearings*, 2185; Kimmel to Stark, 22 August 1941, *Hearings*, 2245. For the Army's situation, see Weigley, *History*, 432-7.

52. James M. Callender, George W. Killen, Maurice J. Gremillion, Survey Questionnaire; Vandegrift, ibid., 86-9.

53. Millett, *Semper*, 346-7.

54. "Are We Ready III - Additional data on Defense Battalions covering period 1 March 1941 to 15 September 1941," 16 September, DPPWPSGC 1940-1, Box 15, RG 127, NA; memoir, Taxis, 55-6; memoir, Paige, 40; memoir, Dessez, 157, 164; memoir, Van Ryzin, 77. George Shultz, Donald Regan, and numerous officers of colonel's rank and higher served as members of defense battalions and anti-aircraft battalions, their successors. Few Marines seem to have been hurt by their service with 7th defense battalion (see Survey Questionnaire). Only Francis Loomis, Jr., believed he had to leave the defense battalion to advance his career (memoir, Loomis, 70-2).

55. Memoir, Paige, 40; memoir, Dessez, 157; memoir, Taxis, 50-1; Robert L. High, Antonio Santaniell, Kenneth Patrick, all in Survey Questionnaire; Hough, ibid., 65. There is some hesitancy among Marines and historians to call any leatherneck unit "elite." See Gordon, "U.S. Marine," 361-373. Although Gordon's article deals primarily with the raider battalions, it can be easily applied to defense battalions. The idea of an "elite" unit in the Corps did not sit well because leathernecks considered the whole Corps to be elite.

56. MGC to CNO, 5 September 1941, DPPWPSGC 1926-42, Box 4, RG 127, NA. Mr. Benis M. Frank, Chief Military Historian of the Marine Corps, also helped clarify this section for me.

57. Holcomb to Henry Leonard, 24 October 1941, Holcomb's Broadcast Transcript, 22 November 1941, both in Holcomb's Papers, PPC, Box 5, MCHC; Vandegrfit to Emile P. Moses, 24 Oct, Moses to Vandegrift, 27 Oct, Vandegrift to Marston, n.d. [November 1941], all in Vandegrift Papers, PPC, Box 2, MCHC.

58. "Study on Defenses and Installations at Outlying Pacific Bases," 21 October 1941, AN 127-77-30, Box 2, NRC.

59. Kimmel to Stark, 26 July 1941, *Hearings*, 2240; Kimmel to Stark, 12 August 1941, *Hearings*, 2243; CINCPAC to OPNav, 29 October 1941, CINCPAC to OPNav, 2 December, 1941, both in AN 127-77-30, Box 2, NRC. Regarding Wake, see Kessler, ibid., 9-10, 23-4, 41-2; John P. S. Devereux, *The Story of Wake Island* (Philadelphia: Lippincott, 1947), 36-9; memoirs, Devereux, 104-5; CNO, memo for MGC, 24 October 1941, MGC, memo for CNO, 28 October 1941, all in AN 127-77-30, Box 1, NRC.

60. Memoirs, Devereux, 107; Heinl, *Soldiers*, 323; Miller, ibid., 292.

61. Kessler, ibid., 23.

62. CINCPAC to OPNav, 28 November 1941, *Hearings*, 2481; Kimmel to Stark, 2 December 1941, *Hearings*, 2253-5; CINCPAC to CNO, 2 December 1941, *Hearings*, 2481-5.

63. Kessler, ibid., 11-12; see also memoirs, Pfeiffer, 179; Kimmel to Stark, 2 December 1941, *Hearings*, 2253-5. In addition, the Survey Questionnaire is rife with finger pointing at the Army, Navy, Congress, and the American public.

64. Memoirs, Devereux, 98.

65. Stark and Marshall, memo for Roosevelt, 27 November 1941, *Hearings*, 1083; Morrison, ibid., 184, 227-9; Baer, ibid., 179.

CONCLUSION NOTES

1. Millett, *Semper*, 346.

2. Odell C. Reid, Survey Questionnaire; Weigley, American, 255; Kajiwara, ibid., 29-31. The sources on the defense of Wake are voluminous. The most recent major work is Robert Cressman, 1995. This book has extensive primary and secondary sources in its bibliography.

3. Gordon, "General," 269; Hough, ibid., 56; Millett, *Semper*, 654.